iCONLOGiC ™

v120815
pc: 262
Print isbn: 1932733841
Print isbn 13: 9781932733846
Digital isbn: 1932733868
Digital isbn 13: 9781932733860

Adobe Captivate 9:
The Essentials

"Skills and Drills" Learning

Kevin Siegel

iCONLOGIC
"Skills and Drills" Learning

Contents

Notes

iCONLOGiC

"Skills and Drills" Learning

About This Book

This Section Contains Information About:

The Author

Kevin Siegel is the founder and president of IconLogic, Inc. He has written hundreds of step-by-step computer training books on applications such as *Adobe Captivate, Adobe RoboHelp, Adobe Presenter, Adobe Technical Communication Suite, Adobe Dreamweaver, Adobe InDesign, Microsoft Word, Microsoft PowerPoint, QuarkXPress,* and *TechSmith Camtasia Studio.*

Kevin spent five years in the U.S. Coast Guard as an award-winning photojournalist and has nearly three decades experience as a print publisher, technical writer, instructional designer, and eLearning developer. He is a certified technical trainer, a veteran classroom instructor, and a frequent speaker at trade shows and conventions.

Kevin holds multiple certifications from companies such as Adobe and CompTIA. You can reach Kevin at **ksiegel@iconlogic.com**.

Book Conventions

I believe that learners learn by doing. With that simple concept in mind, IconLogic books are created by trainers/authors with years of experience training adult learners. Before IconLogic books, our instructors rarely found a book that was perfect for a classroom setting. If the book was beautiful, odds were that the text was too small to read and hard to follow. If the text in a book was the right size, the quality of exercises left something to be desired.

Finally tiring of using inadequate materials, our instructors started teaching without any books at all. Years ago we had many students ask if the in-class instruction came from a book. If so, they said they'd buy the book. That sparked an idea. We asked students—just like you—what they wanted in a training manual. You responded, and that methodology is used in this book and every IconLogic training manual.

This book has been divided into several modules. Because each module builds on lessons learned in a previous module, I recommend that you complete each module in succession. Each module guides you through lessons step-by-step. Here is the lesson key:

❐ instructions for you to follow look like this

If you are expected to type anything or if something is important, it is set in bold type like this:

❐ type **9** into the text field

When you are asked to press a key on your keyboard, the instruction looks like this:

❐ press [**shift**]

I hope you enjoy the book. If you have any comments or questions, please see page xii for our contact information.

Confidence Checks

As you move through the lessons in this book, you will come across the little guy at the right. He indicates a Confidence Check. Throughout each module, you are guided through hands-on, step-by-step exercises. But at some point you'll have to fend for yourself. That is where Confidence Checks come in. Please be sure to complete each of the challenges because some exercises build on completed Confidence Checks.

Book Requirements

This workbook teaches you how to use Adobe Captivate version 9. The Adobe Captivate software does not come with this book. The software can be downloaded directly from Adobe (**www.adobe.com/products/captivate.html**). You do not need to purchase Captivate to learn Captivate; the free trial version of the software can be downloaded via the link above. The only limitation on the trial is that it lasts for 30 days from the day you first run the software on your computer.

Besides a computer and Adobe Captivate 9, here's what else you need to use this book:

Microphone, Speakers, and/or a Headset: During the module on Audio, which begins on page 139, you will learn how to import, record, and edit audio. You will need a microphone and speakers or a headset to complete those activities.

eLearning Assets: Captivate comes with several images (known as Characters) and Themes. To ensure you have all of the assets you need to complete the lessons in this book, download and install the eLearning Assets via the link at **www.adobe.com/cfusion/tdrc/index.cfm?product=captivate**.

NeoSpeech: You will learn how to convert written text into an audio file during activities beginning on page 157. To use the NeoSpeech Text-To-Speech feature, you will need to install the NeoSpeech software after installing Captivate. NeoSpeech comes free with Captivate but is not installed during the Captivate installation process. You can download NeoSpeech from **www.adobe.com/cfusion/tdrc/index.cfm?product=captivate**.

Some people have a hard time finding the eLearning Assets and NeoSpeech download links because they aren't shown in a drop-down menu. Look for this paragraph: "Adobe Captivate 9.0 comes with a wide range of assets which can be used to create great looking eLearning content." You'll find the download link in that paragraph.

Microsoft PowerPoint: PowerPoint 2007 or newer is preferred. PowerPoint, which does not come with Captivate, is used during the PowerPoint integration activities beginning on page 188. If PowerPoint is not installed, you will not be able to complete all of the activities.

Microsoft Word 2007 or newer: Word, which does not come with Captivate, is used during activities beginning on page 237. If Word is not installed, you will not be able to complete all of the activities.

Data Files (Captivate Project Assets)

You're probably chomping at the bit, ready to dive into Captivate and begin creating eLearning lessons. Not so fast... do you have some sample projects? What about graphics? Do you have some sound effects to play with? No? No worries. I've got everything you need—I call them data files—and they can be downloaded from the Iconlogic website for free.

Windows users: Work through the following activity.

Mac users: Skip the following activity and go to the Mac activity on page xi.

Student Activity: Download the Windows Data Files

1. Download the PC student data files necessary to use this book.

   ❑ use a web browser and go to **http://www.iconlogic.com/pc**
   ❑ click the **Captivate 9: The Essentials** link

2. Save the file to your computer. After the file downloads, close the web browser.

3. Extract the data files.

   ❑ find the **Captivate9Data** file you just downloaded to your computer
   ❑ double-click the file to execute it (even though the file is an EXE file, it's not a program; rather it's an archive containing zipped data files)
   ❑ if presented with a Security Warning dialog box click **Run** or **Yes**

   The WinZip Self Extractor opens.

   ❑ confirm **C:** appears in the **Unzip to Folder** area (only change the **Unzip to folder** if you are prohibited from installing assets directly to your C drive)

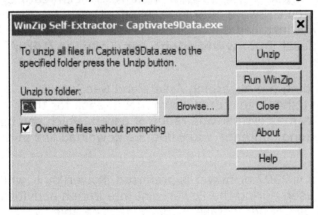

   ❑ click the **Unzip** button

   You are notified that more than 100 files were unzipped.

   ❑ click the **OK** button and then click the **Close** button

   The data files have been installed on your hard drive (within a folder named **Captivate9Data**). As you move through the lessons in this book, you will be working with these files. You can skip the next activity and go to page xii.

Student Activity: Download the Mac Data Files

1. Download the Mac student data files necessary to use this book.

   ❏ use a web browser and go to **http://www.iconlogic.com/mac**
   ❏ click the **Captivate 9: The Essentials** link

   The zipped data files are typically downloaded to the **Downloads** folder on your Mac and are automatically extracted into the folder named **Captivate9Data**.

2. Move the data files folder to your desktop.

   ❏ drag the **Captivate9Data** folder from the **Downloads** folder to your desktop

3. You can now close the **Downloads** folder window and your web browser.

   Before starting the lessons in this book, it's a good idea to review "How Software Updates Affect This Book" on page xii.

How Software Updates Affect This Book

This book was written specifically to teach you how to use **Adobe Captivate version 9.0**. At the time this book was written, Captivate 9 was the latest and greatest version of the Captivate software available from Adobe.

With each major release of Captivate, my intention is to write a new book to support that version and make it available within 30-60 days of the software being released by Adobe. From time to time, Adobe makes service releases/patches of Captivate available for customers that fix bugs or add functionality. For instance, I would expect Adobe to update Captivate with a patch or two within a few months of Captivate 9 being released. That patched version might be called Captivate **9.01** or **9.1**. Usually these updates are minor (bug fixes) and have little or no impact on the lessons presented in this book. However, Adobe sometimes makes significant changes to the way Captivate looks or behaves, even with minor patches. (Such was the case when Adobe updated Captivate from version 5 to 5.5—about a dozen features were added, and a few panels were actually renamed, throwing readers of my books into a tizzy.)

Because it is not possible for me to recall and update printed books, some instructions you are asked to follow in this book may not match the patched/updated version of Captivate that you might be using. If something on your screen does not match what I am showing in the book, please visit the Adobe Captivate 9 product page on my website for possible updates (http://www.iconlogic.com/adobe-captivate-9-essentials-workbook.html).

Contacting IconLogic

IconLogic, Inc.
1582 Indian Bluffs Dr., Maineville, OH, 45039 | 410.956.4949
Web: **www.iconlogic.com** | Email: **info@iconlogic.com**

Special Thanks

AJ Walther contributed to the Preface (beginning on page 1). Specifically, AJ wrote "Designing Slides in Captivate" on page 9, and "Fonts and eLearning" on page 10.

Barbara Ash (www.urgoal.com) provided the **PhotoshopVignette** project you will work with beginning on page 136. Barbara is an Adobe certified instructor and Adobe design specialist. For the past 20 years, she has been teaching Adobe applications and consulting with companies and organizations of all types.

Jill McGillen (www.nextturnconsulting.com) donated the **Introduction** project you will work with beginning on page 84. Jill's company, Next Turn Consulting, is a training company specializing in improving communication, leadership, and results.

Ellie Abrams (ellie@esatraininginc.com) offered her considerable proofreading skills to purge as many grammar errors as possible.

iCONLOGiC

"Skills and Drills" Learning

Rank Your Skills

Before starting this book, complete the skills assessment on the next page.

Skills Assessment

How This Assessment Works

Below you will find 10 course objectives for *Adobe Captivate 9: The Essentials*. **Before starting the book:** Review each objective and rank your skills using the scale next to each objective. A rank of ① means **No Confidence** in the skill. A rank of ⑤ means **Total Confidence**. After you've completed this assessment, go through the entire book. **After finishing the book:** Review each objective and rank your skills now that you've completed the book. Most people see dramatic improvements in the second assessment after completing the lessons in this book.

Before-Class Skills Assessment

1. I can record a Custom Project.	①	②	③	④	⑤
2. I can create a Rollover Slidelet.	①	②	③	④	⑤
3. I can insert a Text Caption.	①	②	③	④	⑤
4. I can add Click Boxes.	①	②	③	④	⑤
5. I can insert Highlight Boxes.	①	②	③	④	⑤
6. I can insert Rollover Captions.	①	②	③	④	⑤
7. I can add Text Entry Boxes.	①	②	③	④	⑤
8. I can create a TOC using the Skin Editor.	①	②	③	④	⑤
9. I can perform a "Round-trip" to Word.	①	②	③	④	⑤
10. I can publish HTML5 output.	①	②	③	④	⑤

After-Class Skills Assessment

1. I can record a Custom Project.	①	②	③	④	⑤
2. I can create a Rollover Slidelet.	①	②	③	④	⑤
3. I can insert a Text Caption.	①	②	③	④	⑤
4. I can add Click Boxes.	①	②	③	④	⑤
5. I can insert Highlight Boxes.	①	②	③	④	⑤
6. I can insert Rollover Captions.	①	②	③	④	⑤
7. I can add Text Entry Boxes.	①	②	③	④	⑤
8. I can create a TOC using the Skin Editor.	①	②	③	④	⑤
9. I can perform a "Round-trip" to Word.	①	②	③	④	⑤
10. I can publish HTML5 output.	①	②	③	④	⑤

IconLogic, Inc.
"Skills and Drills" Learning
Web: www.iconlogic.com | Email: info@iconlogic.com

iCONLOGiC

"Skills and Drills" Learning

Preface

In This Module You Will Learn About:

Education Through Pictures

In a previous life, I was a professional photographer. When I wasn't snapping photos during a five-year tour with the U.S. Coast Guard, I covered media events in New York City as a freelance photographer.

Just about any photographer will tell you that the goal when taking pictures is to capture a story with a few, or maybe just one, photograph. I'm betting that you have heard the saying "a picture is worth a thousand words" more than once. As a professional photographer, I lived those words.

I have spent the bulk of my career attempting to perfect the art of teaching complex concepts to busy, distracted adult learners. I have always attempted to write documentation using as few words as possible and to teach lessons as efficiently as possible.

If you are in the business of educating, you know how difficult the job of writing relevant lesson plans with fewer and fewer words can be. My step-by-step workbooks have long been known for their "skills-and-drills learning" approach. The term "skills-and-drills" learning means different things to different people. For some, it means fast-moving lessons that do not drown a person with unnecessary information. For me, "skills-and-drills learning" means learning something by doing, whatever that something is. It also means learning with a heavy dose of imagery instead of a heavy dose of text.

I learned long ago that people tend to think not with words but with pictures. Here's an example of what I mean.

> *Close your eyes for a second and picture* **three** *in your mind's eye. Open your eyes after a few seconds and read on. (See how precise I am? I know that some of you would have closed your eyes, kept them closed, and then fallen fast asleep without the last instruction.)*

I wasn't specific when I asked you to picture **three** was I? Because I didn't tell you how to picture *three*, it's a good bet that things such as *three cupcakes, three bowls of ice cream,* or *three big boxes of Cap'n Crunch* (everyone knows that the Cap'n is the best breakfast cereal *ever*) flashed into your mind's eye. Maybe a large numeral 3 appeared in your mind's eye—not the word "three." In fact, I doubt that you visualized the word *three*. Why? As I said above, people think in terms of pictures, not words. That's the reason my books usually contain hundreds of screen captures that visually explain a concept that might have taken several paragraphs to explain. And when I do have to explain a concept, I make every effort to minimize the chatter and get right to the point.

RoboDemo to Captivate

A picture can be nice, but it's static. No matter how good a picture is, it is limited in its ability to convey detailed information or concepts. Knowing this limitation, I searched for a program I could use to augment the activities presented in my books. I was specifically looking for a program that would make the lessons in my books come to life and allow me to create software simulations.

Over the years, I have found several programs that I like. The programs capture videos of my computer screen and mouse actions well enough, but the resulting lessons were *huge*. A five-minute eLearning lesson could easily gobble up nearly 100 megabytes of storage space on my web server. Downloading a file that large via the Internet could take a lot of time, even with a fast Internet connection.

Large file sizes were just one part of the problem. The output published by the early eLearning tools were not cross-platform (meaning that they would not work on both Macs and PCs running Windows). And the first eLearning lessons I created were videos that were not capable of being interactive. I firmly believe that *showing* something to learners isn't the same as *teaching* learners a skill and letting them actually *perform* the skill.

Early eLearning technology was so bad that I gave up on the idea and decided to wait until someone came up with a "killer" application. That program began life simply enough as a little utility called Flashcam (by Nexus Concepts, 2002). Flashcam was a simple screen capture application that made quick work of capturing just about anything you could do on your computer. Flashcam soon became the property of eHelp Software and was renamed RoboDemo. At that point, RoboDemo could be used to create sophisticated software demonstrations and interactive simulations.

eHelp Software was responsible for RoboDemo versions 3 through 5. After that, Macromedia (of Dreamweaver and Flash fame) acquired eHelp Software. Macromedia revamped RoboDemo, added even more awesome features, and changed the name of the program from RoboDemo to Captivate.

In 2005, Adobe Systems acquired Macromedia. Hence, the program has been known as *Adobe Captivate*. Adobe's first version of Captivate was Adobe Captivate 2.

If you're totally new to Adobe Captivate, the first thing you need to know is what the program is used to create. Microsoft Word creates documents. Adobe InDesign creates brochures, newspapers, and magazines. Adobe Acrobat creates PDFs. So what's up with Captivate? Using Adobe Captivate, you can create eLearning courses about *anything*! Need to create an online lesson about terrorism awareness? How about a course on conflict resolution? How about a simulation teaching colleagues how to attach a file to an email created in Microsoft Outlook? You can use Captivate to create eLearning for all of these... an endless number of subjects. The eLearning content you create with Captivate can be interactive—you can include text, rollover areas, clickable hotspots, quizzes, typing areas, sound effects, videos, special effects, audio, and more.

Finished Adobe Captivate projects can be published as Flash (SWF), HTML5, Word documents, PDFs, and videos. The lessons you publish can be viewed by a consumer via a Macintosh or a Windows-based PC. Learners can consume your content via a corporate web server, YouTube, Vimeo, mobile device (iPads, iPhones, Android, Kindle Fire, etc.), and even Adobe Reader (if you publish a lesson as a PDF).

Planning eLearning Projects

By the time you finish the last lesson, you should be able to use Captivate to create some compelling, technically sound eLearning lessons. However, publishing technically sound content does not necessarily mean creating *good* eLearning. If you want to create good, useful lessons, you have to plan ahead. Before creating a Captivate project, clarify the following:

❑ Why are you creating an eLearning course in the first place? You'd be surprised how many people start Captivate and just start creating content. This kind of development process might be well-intentioned, but you really need to map out the entire course, including how you are going to track learner comprehension (if that's important to you). During the mapping process, you might come to the conclusion that your course simply isn't appropriate for eLearning and move on to another course.

❑ Who is your audience? The way you teach children is different from the way you teach adults. For instance, children need praise and encouragement during the learning process that an adult learner might find annoying, if not down-right obnoxious.

❑ What exactly are you teaching, and is it appropriate for eLearning? Not every lesson in an instructor-led lesson can be effectively re-tooled as an eLearning lesson. For instance, if a course relies on breakout groups, group discussion, or collaborative work, those aspects of the course cannot be included in eLearning. Keep in mind that eLearners almost always work on their own with little or no interaction with a colleague.

❑ Does your project need to accommodate learners with disabilities? If the answer is yes, you should budget approximately 30 percent more time to produce each lesson. Although it's not difficult to create accessible eLearning, it takes time.

❑ Do you want your projects to contain images and background music? If so, where will you get them? Also, are you going to use a template? If so, who is going to design/create it?

❑ Will there be captions (written instructions and descriptions)? If so, who will write the content for these captions? Do you need an eLearning script? Do you need a voice-over script?

❑ Is your course soft-skills, or is it a software simulation? If it is soft-skills, does it make sense to create most of the content in Microsoft PowerPoint and then import the presentation into Captivate?

eLearning Development Phases

The infographic below offers a visual way to think about the eLearning development process and phases. A larger version of the graphic can be downloaded from www.iconlogic.com/skills-drills-workbooks/elearning-resources.html.

eLearning Development Phases

 1 DISCOVERY

Meet with the client. Find out **what they want** in an ideal eLearning course. Who is the **audience**? Define a course **mission statement** for the course in general. You'll also need a mission statement for each lesson in the course. Will the course require **accessibility**? **Audio**? Will it need to be **localized**? What kind of **hardware** will students be using to access the course?

DESIGN **2**

Which tool will you be using to develop the content (**Captivate**, **PowerPoint**, **Presenter**, **Storyline**, or perhaps a combination of a couple tools)? **Instructional design**, a **graphical treatment**, and **navigational choices** are now made and implemented.

 3 WRITING and/or STORYBOARDING

Now that you have chosen a production tool and decided the overall design of the course, you'll need to **plot out the flow** of the course and **write a script and/or a storyboard**. If the course includes voiceover audio, you'll need a separate (and different) script for that.

PRODUCTION **4**

Now it's time to get busy with the **development work** in the selected tool. This includes everything right up to the point of publishing. You'll also **beta test** the lessons in this phase as they are completed.

 5 CLIENT APPROVAL

You're almost there! But, before project completion, you'll need to get your **client's approval**. Depending upon how this goes, **you may need to repeat parts of steps two, three, and four**.

PUBLISHING and IMPLEMENTATION **6**

This includes not only **publishing locally**, but uploading the content to a **web server** or **LMS (SCORM or AICC)**. Be sure to allow time to work out bugs in this phase.

 7 MAINTENANCE

You did a great job! But sometimes changes and updates are necessary. This phase includes **making updates** to the content and **re-posting to the LMS or web server**.

Brought to you by:

iCONLOGiC
www.iconlogic.com

Budgeting Considerations

Many new eLearning developers underestimate the time needed to produce Captivate projects. Although it is certainly easier and faster to create eLearning content than ever before, it still takes time. To determine your level of effort, the first thing you need to know is how long you want your eLearning course to play (in minutes.) Once you have that number, you can calculate your level of effort.

Let's estimate how long it might to take to create a 60-minute eLearning course. Because you should not create a single Captivate project that, when published, plays for 60 consecutive minutes, it's ideal to break the 60 minutes of content into manageable chunks. I'd suggest that each chunk play for **no more than five minutes**. In that case, you will have 12 Captivate projects, each playing for five-minutes.

You need to design and then write the content for the course so you will need a script and/or storyboard. If there's going to be voice-over audio (I'd encourage you to include voice-over audio), you'll need a voice-over script.

Storyboards are rough sketches that show the general content of your project, slide by slide. If your projects contain more screen shots of an application than captions, a storyboard is a good idea.

Scripts are detailed step-by-step procedures. These are ideal if your project will contain a significant number of Text Captions.

Voice-over scripts are important because you don't want the narrator simply reading aloud the text displayed on the screen. Studies have shown that a narrator simply reading the text being displayed is a distraction to the learner.

It could take at least three hours to write a script to support a five-minute eLearning lesson. Therefore, you should budget at least 36 hours to write the entire one-hour eLearning course (12x3=36). Depending on how fast you write, you could easily double those hours, meaning you may need to budget approximately 80 hours for writing.

When creating content in Captivate, you can and should begin with a project template. A template is essentially a completed shell project that you will use as the basis of all of your projects. It's not difficult to create a template, but it takes time. An ideal template contains placeholders, an introduction slide, transitional slides, a conclusion slide, a skin, and appropriate Start and End Properties (although these terms may seem foreign to you now, you will learn about many of them as you move through the lessons presented in this book).

In my experience, writing a voice-over script is easier than writing a step-by-step script for recording a software simulation (voice-over scripts typically take me 50 percent less time to write). If you spent 80 hours writing the script, you should budget 40 hours to write the voice-over script.

Once the voice-over script is done, you'll also need to include time for recording the audio narration (voice-overs), making corrections to the step-by-step script post-rehearsal, and recording the lessons using Captivate (the recording time should take the same amount of time as the process being recorded).

As I mentioned above, at two hours of production for every minute of eLearning, it could easily take 10 hours to produce a five-minute Captivate lesson. During the production process, you will likely need to add and/or edit text captions (which you will learn about beginning on page 66). Typical Captivate projects include interactive objects, such as Click Boxes (page 179), Buttons (page 32), and Text Entry Boxes (page 183). And a typical project should include a quiz to measure learner comprehension of the content (you will learn about quizzes beginning on page 199).

During the production process, you'll likely add audio clips to the project's background, individual slides, and even objects on individual slides. It's also likely that you'll either record voice-over audio (or use Captivate's Text to Speech feature to convert written text to voice-over audio. And you'll likely need to edit the audio files by performing such common tasks as removing unwanted noise. (You will learn to work with audio on page 139.)

Finally, you'll need to publish the finished project into any one of several output formats, possibly uploading those files to a server or Learning Management System (LMS) and testing for scoring or interactivity errors. After that, you'll need to fix problems (and there will likely be plenty of problems that need to be fixed). After fixing those problems, you'll need to republish, repost, and then retest. (You will learn to Publish projects beginning on page 225.)

Your eLearning development budget (to create a 60-minute eLearning course) might look something like this:

- ❏ 40-80 hours to write an eLearning script or create the storyboard to support 12, five-minute lessons for a one-hour course.

- ❏ 120 hours to edit, produce, and test 12, five-minute lessons (two-hours for every minute of playtime).

- ❏ 20-40 hours to write a narration script to be used by your narrator.

- ❏ 20-40 hours to record and enhance voice narration (less if you use Text to Speech, which you will learn about on page 157).

Project Size and Display Resolution

When you create a blank Captivate project or record a software simulation, you'll need to set the project's width and height. For instance, in the second module (page 24), you create a blank project and set its size to 800 x 600. That size is perfectly fine for learners who access your content via a desktop computer with a typical monitor (typical meaning a 15-17 inch monitor).

Several years ago, monitors were small and display resolutions were low. In fact, a display resolution of 800 x 600 pixels was common. If you developed eLearning content for a display that small, a project size of 640 x 480 was ideal. A few years later, 1024 x 768 was the standard display resolution, resulting in typical eLearning lessons sized to 800 x 600.

According to **w3schools.com**, the standard desktop screen resolution today is 1366 x 768, and it's trending higher. (You'll find that available resolutions vary from system to system. For instance, I use an HP 22-inch display that doesn't support 1366 x 768. Instead, my closest options are 1360 x 768 and 1376 x 812.)

Because screen resolutions are higher than ever, many eLearning developers are seeking an optimal viewing experience for learners. But what's the ideal size for an eLearning lesson? Unfortunately, there isn't a cookie-cutter answer. The size of the lesson you create depends largely on the size of your display and its resolution. If you are recording a software simulation, the size of your project might be dependent upon the size of the software you're recording (some software cannot be resized and may to take up your whole display).

There's more to consider when it comes to project size. What kind of device are your learners using? How big is their display? Is their device typically used vertically (portrait) or horizontally (landscape)? What is the typical size of an iPad? How about a Surface Pro?

If you are creating content for learners using standard desktop computers (Windows or Mac), your 800 x 600 project might look fine. However, if you upload your content to YouTube, 800 x 600 won't look right (you will see black bars on one or both sides of the video, and the video might look distorted during playback).

Selecting an ideal project size is a delicate balancing act between the size of the capture area and an ideal screen resolution. When I create YouTube videos, I set Captivate's recording size to 1280 x 720 and my computer's screen resolution fairly high. Although I could go higher with my screen resolution and capture more of my screen, the captured screen text at a higher screen resolution tends to be small and difficult for most people to read.

When the time comes to Publish your Captivate project, there is an option called **Scalable HTML content**.

☑ Scalable HTML content

When you publish your project with Scalable HTML content enabled, learners with large screens similar to yours will see your lesson pretty much at full size. For other learners, the lesson will automatically scale up or down to fit their screen. In short, Scalable HTML content takes away much of the anxiety you'll have to contend with when it comes to project size. For that reason, I encourage you to ensure that Scalable HTML Content is always enabled when publishing. (When developing your eLearning course, consider using a font and font size that remains readable when small. Imagine how tiny the text could become if a learner uses a smart phone.)

Designing Slides in Captivate

As you begin to work in Captivate to develop standard (not video) projects, the program will likely seem very familiar to you... sort of like Microsoft PowerPoint. If you've used PowerPoint you are familiar with the Filmstrip showing miniatures of the slides along the left side of the PowerPoint interface. Captivate is similar. In fact, like PowerPoint, you create individual slides in Captivate and populate those slides with text, images, animation... just about anything.

You don't have to be a seasoned designer to produce beautiful and effective Captivate slides. Here are a few tips to get you started:

❏ There are occasions when a bulleted list is the best way to convey an idea. Although PowerPoint uses a bulleted approach to information by default, you do not have to use that format in eLearning.

❏ Try splitting the bullets into separate slides with a single image to illustrate each point, or forgo the text altogether and replace it with a chart, diagram, or other informative image.

❏ It is not necessary to have every bit of information you cover on one slide. Encourage your audience to listen and, if necessary, take notes based on what you say, not what is shown on the slide.

❏ Nothing says "High School Presentation Circa 1997" quite like a dancing animated image clumsily plopped on a rainbow gradient background with a big, garish image.

❏ Few learners are impressed with how many moving, colorful objects each slide contains. When it comes to eLearning, the old saying, "content is King," has never been more appropriate. Ensure each of your slides contains relevant, need-to-know information and that the information is presented as clutter-free as possible.

❏ Consider taking more of a photographic approach to the images you use. You can easily find stock photographs on the web using any one of a number of pay-for-use websites. There are many free sites, but keep in mind that to save time and frustration (and improve on the selection and quality), you might want to set aside a budget to pay for images.

Fonts and eLearning

There is no denying that the most important thing about eLearning is solid content. But could you be inadvertently making your content harder to read and understand by using the wrong fonts? Is good font selection really important? Read on to discover the many surprising ways fonts can affect your content.

Some Fonts Read Better On-Screen

eCommerce Consultant Dr. Ralph F. Wilson did a study in 2001 to determine if serif fonts (fonts with little lines on the tops and bottoms of characters, such as Times New Roman) or sans serif fonts (those without lines, such as Arial) were more suited to being read on computer monitors. His study concluded that although Times New Roman is easily read in printed materials, the lower resolution of monitors (72 dots per inch (dpi) versus 180 dpi or higher) makes it much more difficult to read in digital format. Arial 12 pt was pitted against Times New Roman 12 pt with respondents finding the sans serif Arial font more readable at a rate of two to one.

Lorem ipsum frangali puttuto rigali fortuitous confulence magficati alorem. Lorem ipsum frangali puttuto rigali fortuitous confulence magficati alorem.	Lorem ipsum frangali puttuto rigali fortuitous confulence magficati alorem. Lorem ipsum frangali puttuto rigali fortuitous confulence magficati alorem.
Times New Roman 12 pt	Arial 12 pt
520	1123
32%	68%

Source: http://www.wilsonweb.com/wmt6/html-email-fonts.htm

Wilson also tested the readability of Arial versus Verdana on computer screens and found that in font sizes greater than 10 pt, Arial was more readable, whereas Verdana was more readable in font sizes 10 pt and smaller.

So should you stop using Times New Roman in your eLearning lessons? Not completely. For instance, you can still use Times New Roman for text content that is not expected to be skimmed over quickly or read in a hurry.

Some Fonts Increase Trust

A 2008 study by Sharath Sasidharan and Ganga Dhanesh for the Association of Information Systems found that typography can affect trust in eCommerce. The study found that to instill trust in online consumers, you should keep it simple: "To the extent possible, particularly for websites that need to engage in financial transactions or collect personal information from their users, the dominant typeface used to present text material should be a serif or sans serif font such as Times New Roman or Arial."

If you feel your eLearning content will be presented to a skeptical audience (or one you've never worked with before), dazzling them with fancy fonts may not be the way to go. You can use fancy fonts from time to time to break up the monotony of a dry lesson, but consider using such non-standard fonts sparingly. Use the fancy fonts for headings or as accents but not for the bulk of your text.

The Readability of Fonts Affects Participation

A study done at the University of Michigan in 2008 on typecase in instructions found that the ease with which a font in instructional material is read can have an impact on the perceived skill level needed to complete a task.

The study found that if directions are presented in a font that is deemed more difficult to read, "the task will be viewed as being difficult, taking a long time to complete and perhaps, not even worth trying."

The results of the study by Wilson indicate that it is probably not a good idea to present eLearning material, especially to beginners, in a Times New Roman font, as it may make the information seem too difficult to process or overwhelming.

Popular eLearning Fonts

I polled my "Skills & Drills" newsletter readers and asked which fonts they tended to use in eLearning. Here is a list of the most popular fonts:

- ❑ Verdana
- ❑ Helvetica
- ❑ Arial
- ❑ Calibri
- ❑ Times
- ❑ Palatino
- ❑ Times New Roman
- ❑ Century Schoolbook (for print)

Fonts and Personas

If you are creating eLearning for business professionals, you might want to use a different font in your design than you would if you were creating eLearning for high school students. But what font would you use if you want to convey a feeling of happiness? Formality? Cuddliness?

In a study (funded by Microsoft) by A. Dawn Shaikh, Barbara S. Chaparro, and Doug Fox, the perceived personality traits of fonts were categorized. The table below shows the top three fonts for each personality objective.

	Top Three		
Stable	TNR	Arial	Cambria
Flexible	Kristen	Gigi	Rage Italic
Conformist	Courier New	TNR	Arial
Polite	Monotype Corsiva	TNR	Cambria
Mature	TNR	Courier New	Cambria
Formal	TNR	Monotype Corsiva	Georgia
Assertive	Impact	Rockwell Xbold	Georgia
Practical	Georgia	TNR	Cambria
Creative	Gigi	Kristen	Rage Italic
Happy	Kristen	Gigi	Comic Sans
Exciting	Gigi	Kristen	Rage Italic
Attractive	Monotype Corsiva	Rage Italic	Gigi
Elegant	Monotype Corsiva	Rage Italic	Gigi
Cuddly	Kristen	Gigi	Comic Sans
Feminine	Gigi	Monotype Corsiva	Kristen
Unstable	Gigi	Kristen	Rage Italic
Rigid	Impact	Courier New	Agency FB
Rebel	Gigi	Kristen	Rage Italic
Rude	Impact	Rockwell Xbold	Agency FB
Youthful	Kristen	Gigi	Comic Sans
Casual	Kristen	Comic Sans	Gigi
Passive	Kristen	Gigi	Comic Sans
Impractical	Gigi	Rage Italic	Kristen
Unimaginative	Courier New	Arial	Consolas
Sad	Impact	Courier New	Agency FB
Dull	Courier New	Consolas	Verdana
Unattractive	Impact	Courier New	Rockwell Xbold
Plain	Courier New	Impact	Rockwell Xbold
Coarse	Impact	Rockwell Xbold	Courier New
Masculine	Impact	Rockwell Xbold	Courier New

Source: http://usabilitynews.org/perception-of-fonts-perceived-personality-traits-and-uses/

Module 1: Exploring Captivate

In This Module You Will Learn About:

- The Captivate Interface, page 14
- Previewing, page 21

And You Will Learn To:

- Explore a Finished Captivate Project, page 14
- Zoom and Magnify, page 16
- Navigate a Project, page 17
- Explore and Reset the Workspace, page 19
- Preview the Entire Project, page 21

The Captivate Interface

As you work through the lessons in this book, the goal is to get you comfortable with each specific Captivate area or feature before proceeding. Like any feature-rich program, mastering Captivate is going to be a marathon, not a sprint. Soon enough you'll be in full stride, creating awesome eLearning content using Captivate. But before the sprint comes the crawl. During these first few activities, I'd like to give you a chance to familiarize yourself with Captivate's user interface. Specifically, you'll be instructed to start Captivate, open an existing project, and poke around Captivate's interface a bit.

Student Activity: Explore a Finished Captivate Project

1. Start Adobe Captivate.

   The process of starting a program varies slightly from operating system to operating system. Because Captivate is available for both the Macintosh and Windows, I'll leave it to you to start the program using any technique you're comfortable with.

   Once Captivate starts, you'll see the **Home** screen consisting of two tabs: **Recent** and **New**. The Recent tab will be blank until after you have opened or created a project. Shown below is the Macintosh version of Adobe Captivate 9.

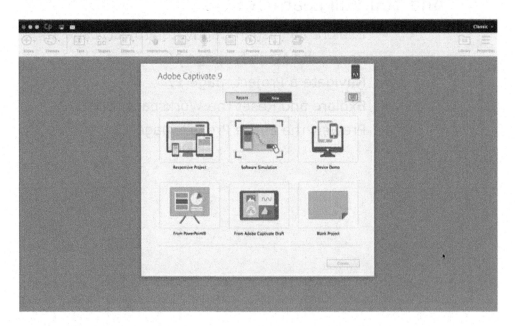

   Captivate is nearly identical on the Windows and Macintosh operating systems. Nevertheless, there are some differences between the two versions, and I'll point them out as you work through this book.

   Note: You are about to open a Captivate project from the group of assets (data files) that support the lessons in this book. If you have not yet downloaded and installed the **Captivate9Data** files, turn to the **About This Book Section** and complete the "Data Files (Captivate Project Assets)" activity that begins on page x before moving on to the next step.

2. Open a project from the **Captivate9Data** folder.

❑ click the **Recent** tab

❑ from the bottom left of the tab, click the **Browse** button

The **Open** dialog box appears.

❑ navigate to the **Captivate9Data** folder and open **AceInterview.cptx**

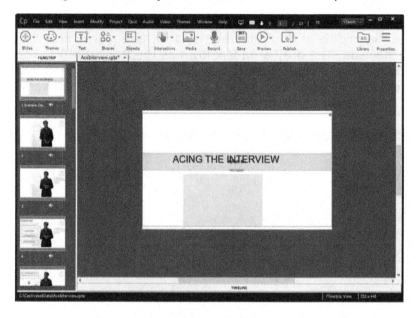

3. Close the project and reopen it using the Recent tab.

❑ choose **File > Close** (do not save the project if prompted)

The Captivate Home screen has two tabs: New and Recent. Once you've opened and then closed a project, the Recent tab gives you quick access to those recently used projects.

❑ on the **Home** screen, click the **Recent** tab

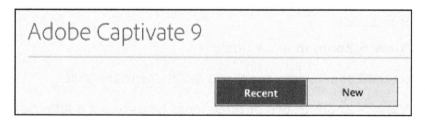

❑ double-click **AceInterview** to reopen the project

Note: Alternatively, you can open existing Captivate projects via **File > Open** or click the **Browse** button on the **Recent** tab.

Student Activity: Zoom and Magnify

1. Ensure that the **AceInterview** project is still open.

2. Zoom away from a slide.

   ☐ choose **View > Magnification > 50%**

   You can zoom as far away as 25 percent and as up close and personal as 400 percent. At a 50 percent view, it's a good bet you can see the Filmstrip at the left, a slide in the middle of the Captivate window, and a gray area surrounding the slide. The gray area is known as the **Pasteboard**. You can drop any slide object on the Pasteboard and leave it there indefinitely. When an object is on the Pasteboard, it will not appear in the published version of your lesson, nor will it preview (you'll learn to both publish and preview later).

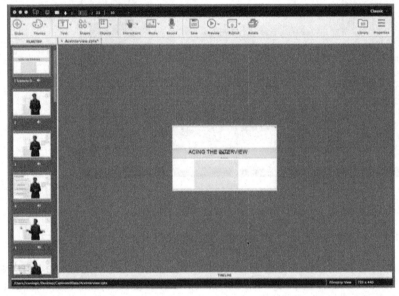

The Pasteboard is the gray space you see surrounding the slide. You can drop slide objects here until you are ready to use them.

3. Zoom closer to a slide.

   ☐ choose **View > Zoom in** a few times

   As you select the Zoom in command, you get closer to the slide.

   ☐ choose **View > Zoom in** two or three more times to get a little closer to the slide

4. Change the slide zoom to Best Fit.

   ☐ choose **View > Magnification > Best Fit**

   Depending on the size of the Captivate window on your computer screen, and your monitor's display resolution, the best Best Fit command is an ideal view when working within Captivate.

Student Activity: Navigate a Project

1. Ensure that the AceInterview project is still open.

2. Switch slides using the Filmstrip.

   ❑ at the left of the Captivate window, scroll up or down the **Filmstrip** as necessary until you see the thumbnail view of slide **7**

   ❑ on the **Filmstrip**, click one time on slide **7** to view the slide in the middle of the Captivate window

Once a slide is open in the main area of the Captivate window, you can select any of the slide's objects and manipulate them. For instance, you can edit slide text, add images, delete images, add a button, change an object's timing, etc. If you need to change the attributes of one or more slides, you do not need to have it open within the main Captivate interface. Instead, you can select one or more slides on the Filmstrip and change their Properties at one time.

3. Jump to a slide using the Go to slide field.

   ❑ from the Captivate menu bar at the top of the window, highlight the number you see in the current slide field

   ❑ type any slide number between **1** and **23**

Note: If you don't see the Page Number field as shown in the image above, try enlarging the Captivate window. When the Captivate window is small, some menu items are cropped from view.

4. Jump between slides using your keyboard.

☐ with any of the slides on the Filmstrip selected, press either [**page up**] or [**page down**] on your keyboard

As you press the keys, notice that you quickly move from slide to slide.

Note: If you are using a Macintosh laptop, such as a MacBook Pro without [**page up**] or [**page down**] keys, try pressing the **up** and **down** arrows on the lower right of your keyboard to move from slide to slide.

Student Activity: Explore and Reset the Workspace

1. Ensure that the AceInterview project is still open.

2. Explore the Properties Inspector and the Library.

   ❏ from the top right of the Captivate window, click **Properties**

   A panel opens at the right of the Captivate window. As you move through the lessons in this book, you'll be using this area frequently. I've heard people refer to Captivate panels by all kinds of names. Is it a pod? Is it a panel? Is it Superman? (I just dated myself with that one.) I promise that there won't be a test about this stuff later, so pick a name for these Captivate areas that works for you. According to my contact at Adobe, each panel is known as an Inspector, so clicking Properties actually displays two inspectors: **Properties** and **Timing**.

   ❏ from the top right of the Captivate window, click **Library**

   The Library Inspector, which keeps tabs of many of a project's assets, takes the place of the Properties Inspector. You'll learn to use the Library beginning on page 90.

   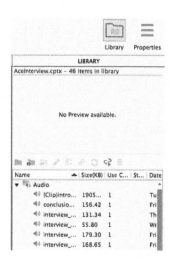

3. Explore the Timeline.

   ☐ from the bottom center of the Captivate window, click **Timeline**

   The Timeline appears at the bottom of the Captivate window. You'll learn how to work with the Timeline beginning on page 76.

With the Timeline and Library open, your screen is a bit more... complicated. Although all of these open inspectors are useful, it's a good idea to know how to get yourself back to the nice, clean interface you saw a few moments ago. Next you'll learn how to reset the workspace.

4. Reset the workspace.

   ☐ choose **Window > Workspace > Reset 'Classic'**

   You can Reset your workspace at any time and as often as you like. If you ever feel that the Captivate interface is getting out of control, you can reset the workspace at any time.

Previewing

You will learn how to create a series of eLearning lessons using Captivate. At some point, you will finish the development process by publishing (you will learn how to Publish beginning on page 225). Once published, the eLearning lesson can be used (consumed) by people using all kinds of devices (including desktop computers and mobile devices, such as the iPad or the Kindle Fire). Prior to publishing, it's a good idea to preview the project so you can see how the lesson looks once published. There are multiple preview options, including Play Slide, Project, From this Slide, Next 5 slides, In Browser, HTML5 in Browser, and In Adobe Edge Inspect. Because previewing the Project shows a quick version of a published project without starting a web browser and Next 5 slides quickly shows just a few slides at a time, I find those two options to be the most useful.

Student Activity: Preview the Entire Project

1. Ensure that the **AceInterview** project is still open.

2. Preview the project.

   ☐ from the **Toolbar** at the top of the Captivate window, click **Preview**

   ☐ choose **Project** from the menu

The lesson is generated and then begins to play. After several seconds, the fourth slide stops and waits for you to interact with it.

Previewing Confidence Check

1. Continue working through the preview.

2. When you are finished interacting with the lesson (you do not need to watch it in its entirety), click the **End** button on the toolbar at the top of the preview.

3. Preview the project **In Browser**.

   A preview of the lesson (as it will appear via a web browser) opens in your default web browser.

4. Again, there is no need to go through the entire lesson. You can close the browser window when you are done exploring.

5. Close the project (there is no need to save if prompted).

   Note: You might have noticed that you cannot drag the Inspectors around your screen like you can in other programs. Because there are so many Inspectors in Captivate, it's generally a good idea to leave the Captivate interface alone. However, if you have multiple monitors, you might want to put a few Inspectors on one monitor and your main Captivate window on another monitor. If you'd like to move your Inspectors around the screen, you can create custom workspaces. Open Captivate's Preferences dialog box by choosing **Edit > Preferences** (if you're a Windows user) or **Adobe Captivate > Preferences** (if you're a Mac user). Then select **Enable custom workspaces/panel undocking**.

   ☑ Enable custom workspaces/panel undocking

   Click the **OK** button to close the dialog box and then restart Captivate. You'll then be able to move several of the panels around your screen (even across multiple screens). If you like your new workspace, you can keep it by choosing **Window > Workspace > Save Workspace**. Once saved, your new workspace is available in the Workspace sub-menu.

   While custom workspaces are great, they can result in a cluttered Captivate environment. For that reason, I'll avoid them completely in this book. I'd encourage you to work through this book using the Classic workspace and create custom workspaces once you feel more comfortable with Adobe Captivate.

iCONLOGiC

"Skills and Drills" Learning

Module 2: New Projects

In This Module You Will Learn About:

And You Will Learn To:

Soft Skills eLearning

You can use Adobe Captivate to record actions you perform on your computer. Those recordings can be interactive (often referred to as "Let Me Try" eLearning), demos (often referred to as "Show Me" eLearning), and videos (much like the kind you've likely seen on YouTube or Vimeo).

Soft Skills eLearning encompasses anything that doesn't fall into the category of a computer recording. Over the years, I've helped my clients develop soft skills lessons covering all kinds of topics, including onboarding, terrorism awareness, compliance training, conflict resolution, and policies and procedures. Anything that's a life skill would fall into the category of soft skills.

During the lessons in this module, you will create a soft skills lesson that introduces employees of an imaginary company called Super Simplistic Solutions. The managers you will add to the lesson don't exist either. Made-up content or not, the project you are about to create will include multiple slides, text captions, and images. You will add interactive buttons to the slides, allowing the learner to move through the lesson at their own pace.

Student Activity: Create a Blank Project

1. Create a blank project.

   ☐ using Adobe Captivate, choose **File > New Project > Blank Project**

   The New Blank Project dialog box opens.

2. Specify a Width and Height for the project.

   ☐ from the **Select** drop-down menu, choose **800 x 600**

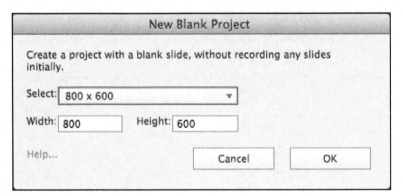

   ☐ click the **OK** button

   The new project is created. It contains only a single slide.

3. Save the new project.

   ☐ choose **File > Save**

   ☐ name the project **OurManagers** and save it to the **Captivate9Data** folder

4. Apply a theme.

❑ from the left side of the **Toolbar**, click **Themes**

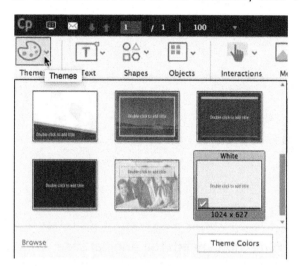

A theme is a collection of master slides, placeholders, and object styles that allow you to keep your slides looking consistent throughout a project. By applying a theme, each new slide you add during the next steps is formatted using the attributes of that theme.

❑ roll your cursor over the themes to display their names and select the one called **Clear**

Note: If you don't see the Clear theme, click the **Browse** link in the lower left of the Themes area and find the themes collection on your computer. Windows users, browse to **eLearning Assets\Layouts\9_0\en_US**. Mac users, browse to **Documents\My Adobe Captivate Projects\Layouts\9_0\en_US**.

You will be prompted to confirm the action.

❑ click the **Yes** button

The existing slide takes on the appearance of the theme.

5. Insert a new slide.

   ❑ choose **Insert > New Slide From > Content 07**

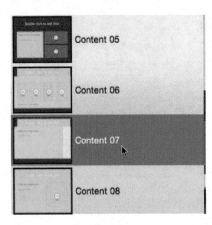

A new slide is inserted on the Filmstrip beneath the original slide. This slide is based on the **Content 7** master slide and contains a few placeholders for a title and subtitle.

6. Delete a slide.

   ❑ on the **Filmstrip** (at the left of the Captivate window), right-click the first slide and choose **Delete**

You'll be prompted to confirm the deletion.

   ❑ click the **OK** button

7. Add content to slide placeholders.

☐ on the slide, double-click the title placeholder where it says "Double click to add title" and replace the placeholder text with **Our Management Team**

☐ double-click the subtitle placeholder where it says "Double click to add subtitle" and replace the placeholder text with **by "Your Full Name"** (type your name in place of the text in quotes)

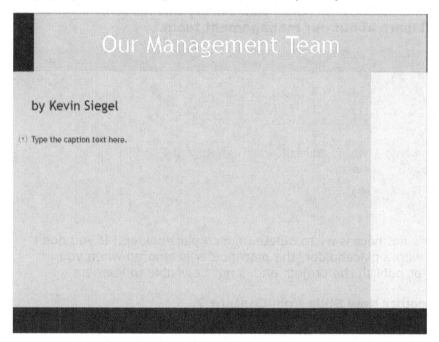

New Slides Confidence Check

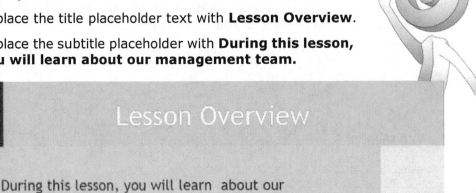

1. Still working in the OurManagers project, insert a **New Slide** from **Content 7**. (Hint: **Insert > New Slide from**.)

2. Replace the title placeholder text with **Lesson Overview**.

3. Replace the subtitle placeholder with **During this lesson, you will learn about our management team.**

Note: It's not necessary to delete unused placeholders. If you don't interact with a placeholder, the placeholder is ignored when you preview or publish the project and is not be visible to learners.

4. Insert another **New Slide** from **Content 7**.

5. Replace the title placeholder text with **Lesson Review**.

6. Replace the subtitle placeholder with **During this lesson, you learned about our key managers.**

7. Replace the caption placeholder with **In particular, you learned that while Biff takes credit for making the company the most successful of its kind in the world, it's really Betty that deserves all of the credit.**

Student Activity: Add Images to Placeholders

1. Ensure that the **OurManagers** project is still open.

2. Insert a slide with an image placeholder.

   ❏ on the Filmstrip, select slide **2**

   ❏ choose **Insert > New Slide from > Content 08**

   The new slide is inserted after the selected Filmstrip slide.

   ❏ ensure you are working on the new slide and replace the title with **Biff Bifferson**

   ❏ replace the subtitle with **President**

   ❏ replace the caption text with **Biff founded the company in 1993 with just $55 in the bank. Today, the company is worth in excess of $10 billion**.

3. Insert an image into an image placeholder.

   ❏ at the right side of the slide, click the **plus sign** in the **Image Placeholder**

   The **Select Image from Library** dialog box opens.

❏ at the left of the dialog box, click the **Import** button

❏ from the **Captivate9Data** folder, open **images_animation**

❏ open the **biff_baby** image

Your slide should look like the image below.

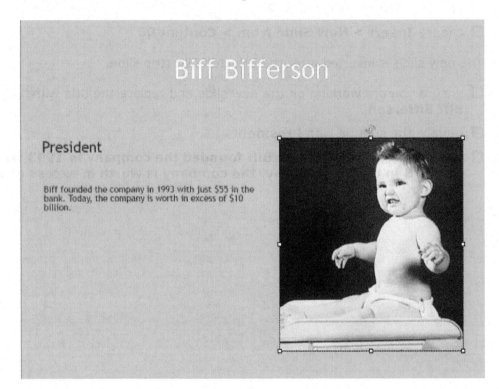

Themes Confidence Check

1. Select slide **3** and insert a new slide based on **Content 04**.

2. Replace the placeholders as necessary to make the new slide look like the image below. (The image used in the image placeholder is **betty_baby**.)

3. Preview the project **In Browser**. (You learned how to Preview on page 21.)

   The lesson automatically moves from slide to slide. When the lesson is finished, you can use the playbar at the bottom of the window to rewind the lesson.

   If this is the first eLearning lesson you've ever created, congratulations are in order. Although this lesson isn't very complex, it is an eLearning lesson. Take a bow... you're on your way!

   In the next section, you'll learn how to add a button to the slides that will add interactivity for the learners and allow them to control when it's time to move from one slide to the next.

4. When finished previewing, close the browser window.

5. Spend a few moments applying a few of the other Themes to your project and take note of how the Theme designs impact your current slide layouts.

6. When finished, **save** and **close** the project.

Buttons

Buttons provide learner interactivity to a slide. Using **Actions**, you can control what happens when the learner successfully clicks a button (such as **Go to the next slide** or **Play Audio**). There are multiple types of buttons: Text, Transparent, Image, and Shapes. During the following activities, you'll insert and format Text buttons.

Student Activity: Insert and Format a Text Button

1. Using Captivate, open **ButtonMe** from the **Captivate9Data** folder.

   With the exception of the Theme and some of the wording on the slides, this is the same project you created earlier.

2. Insert a Text button.

   ❏ ensure that you are on slide **1**

   ❏ from the toolbar, click **Interactions** and choose **Button**

   The new button appears in the middle of the slide. The appearance of the button is based on the fonts and colors used by the selected theme. (This project uses the Blackboard theme.)

3. Drag the button until its position is similar to the picture below.

   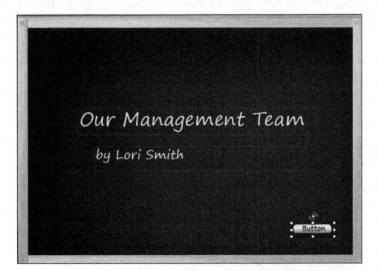

Note: The image above was taken from the Macintosh version of Captivate. If you're using Windows, the font shown on your button looks different than what is shown. No worries. The font used by the button is not important at this point. You'll learn to use Object Styles to control fonts later.

4. Change the text displayed on the button.

   ❏ double-click the button to display the **Properties Inspector**

   Approximately one-third down the Properties Inspector, notice that there are three tabs: **Style**, **Actions**, and **Options**.

   ❏ on the **Style** tab, replace the existing **Caption** text with **Continue**

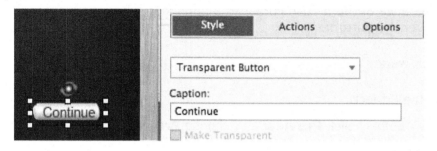

5. Review the button's Action.

   ❏ with the button still selected, select the **Actions** tab on the Properties Inspector

   An Action occurs after the learner has performed a desired step. In this instance, when the learner successfully clicks the button on slide 1, you want the learner to be taken to the next slide. Therefore, the **On Success** action of **Go to the next slide** is perfect.

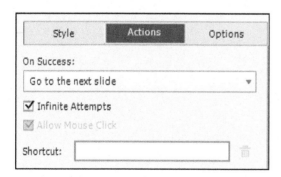

6. Add a Hand Cursor to the button.

   ❒ ensure that the button is still selected

   ❒ on the **Actions** tab, **Others** area, select **Hand Cursor**

> **Others**
> ☐ Pause for Success/Failure Captions
> ☑ Hand Cursor
> ☐ Double-click
> ☐ Disable Click Sound

A Hand Cursor lets the learner know that the button is clickable by changing the appearance of the mouse cursor to a hand icon when the learner runs the mouse over the button.

7. Save your work.

8. Preview the Project.

   ❒ on the Toolbar, click **Preview** and choose **Project**

As the first slide plays, notice that the button prevents the slide from moving forward on its own.

   ❒ click the button to move to the second slide

Did you notice that there was a click sound that accompanied the button? Some people like the click sound, others do not. Assuming you do not like the click sound, you will learn how to remove it.

9. Close the preview.

Student Activity: Disable Click Sounds

1. Ensure that the **ButtonMe** project is still open.

2. Disable a button's Click Sound.

   ❑ ensure that you are on slide **1**

   ❑ double-click the **Button**

   ❑ from the **Actions** tab, **Others** area of the **Properties Inspector**, select **Disable Click Sound**

   > **Others**
   >
   > ☐ Pause for Success/Failure Captions
   >
   > ☑ Hand Cursor
   >
   > ☐ Double-click
   >
   > ☑ Disable Click Sound

3. Preview the Project.

   ❑ on the Toolbar, click **Preview** and choose **Project**

   ❑ click the button to move to the second slide

   Upon clicking the button, notice that the click sound has been removed.

4. Close the preview.

Buttons Confidence Check

1. Still working in the ButtonMe project, copy the button you added to slide 1 to the clipboard.

2. On the Filmstrip, select slide **2**.

3. Press the [**shift**] key on your keyboard, click the **last slide** on the Filmstrip, and then release the [**shift**] key.

   All of the slides except slide 1 should now be selected.

4. Paste the button onto the selected slides.

   The cool thing about copying and pasting slide objects is that, in addition to getting the object on several slides at once, the pasted objects are all in the same slide location.

5. Go to slide **3**.

6. The Continue button is very close to the picture of Biff. You could leave it where it is. However, if you'd like to move it to the other side of the slide, try this technique: select the button and, with the [**shift**] key down, press the [**left arrow key**] on your keyboard several times to move the button left. You can position the button anywhere on the left side of the slide.

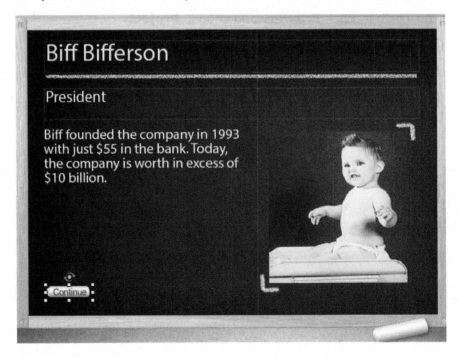

Note: Holding the [**shift**] key down while you press the arrow key moves the object faster than pressing the arrow key repeatedly.

7. Go to slide **5** and select the **Continue** button.

8. Change the button's caption to **Replay**. (You learned how to change a button's caption on page 33.)

9. Change the **On Success** Action for the button to **Jump to slide**.

10. Select **1 Slide 1** as the destination. (You learned about Actions on page 33.)

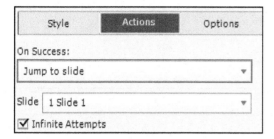

11. Preview the project.

There should be interactive buttons on each slide allowing you to control how fast or slow you move through the lesson. When you get to the last slide, click the Replay button to get to the first slide.

12. Close the preview.

13. Save and close the project.

Notes

iCONLOGiC

"Skills and Drills" Learning

Module 3: Recording Screen Actions

In This Module You Will Learn About:

And You Will Learn To:

Preparing to Record

Standard Captivate projects consist of individual slides, similar to Microsoft PowerPoint. You can create a blank Captivate project and insert slides, just like you learned to do beginning on page 24. If you need to capture a software application, you can use any one of several programs. For instance, I used SnagIt for the Macintosh (**www.snagit.com**) and FullShot (**www.fullshot.com**) for Windows to create the Captivate screen captures in this book. Individual screen captures can be inserted onto any Captivate slide as an image.

As an alternative to using a third-party application to create screen captures, you can use Captivate to record just about anything you do on your computer. Captivate offers three recording types: Automatic, Manual, and Video. If you use Captivate's Automatic recording type, Captivate captures the steps you take on your computer by creating a screen capture every time you click your mouse. There are four Automatic capture modes: Demonstration, Assessment Simulation, Training Simulation, and Custom. Each mode is covered during this module.

If you create projects using the Manual recording type, you are responsible for pressing a specific key on your keyboard each time you want Captivate to create a screen capture (the default key is the Print Screen key in Windows). The problem with recording projects using the Manual Recording method is that you need to be very diligent about pressing the screen capture key on your keyboard. You could easily get distracted and forget to capture important screens, rendering your recording useless and requiring you to recapture some or all of your clicks.

Using the Video recording type, Captivate does not capture individual screens like the Automatic and Manual types. Instead, when the capture process is finished, you end up with a single video demonstrating everything you have done during the recording process. A video recording is ideal if you are trying to create an eLearning lesson demonstrating complex mouse actions (like those that would be required when drawing a shape in an image-editing application). However, editing a video is more limited as compared to editing individual screen captures typical in projects created using the Automatic or Manual recording types.

In the images below, both the Automatic and Manual recording types are shown at the left. Video mode is shown at the right. (**Note:** The Automatic and Manual modes are covered in this book. Video projects are covered in "*Adobe Captivate 9: Beyond the Essentials*.")

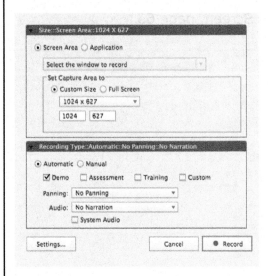
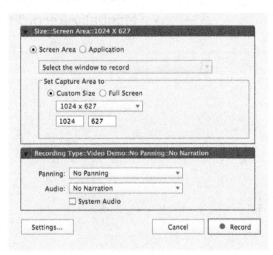

Rehearsals

You have been hired to create an eLearning course that teaches new employees at your company how to use **Notepad** (Windows) or **TextEdit** (Macintosh). One of the lessons you plan to record using Captivate includes how to change the page orientation within Notepad or TextEdit.

Here is a sample script showing the kind of detailed, step-by-step instructions you need to create or receive from a Subject Matter Expert (SME). You are expected to perform each step written below in either Notepad or TextEdit.

Dear Captivate developer, using either Notepad or TextEdit, record the process of changing the Page Orientation from Portrait to Landscape, and then back again (from Landscape to Portrait). Create the recording using a capture size of 800 x 600. Thanks. Your pal, the Subject Matter Expert.

1. Click the File menu.

2. Click the Page Setup menu item.

3. Click the Landscape orientation button.

4. Click the OK button.

5. Click the File menu.

6. Click the Page Setup menu item.

7. Click the Portrait orientation button.

8. Click the OK button.

9. Stop the recording process.

The script sounds simple. However, you will not know what kind of trouble you are going to get into unless you rehearse the script prior to recording the process with Captivate. Let's run a rehearsal, just as if you were a big-time movie director and you were in charge of a blockbuster movie.

Places everyone... and quiet on the set...

Student Activity: Rehearse a Script

1. Minimize (hide) Captivate.

2. Start either Notepad (Windows) or TextEdit (Mac).

   The process of starting either Notepad or TextEdit varies slightly, depending on your operating system. For instance, if you are using Windows 7, choose **Start**, type **notepad**, and press [**enter**]. If you are using Windows 8 or newer, use the **Search** feature to start Notepad. If you are using a Mac, choose **Go > Applications**. Locate and then open **TextEdit**, and then create a New document.

   In the images below, Notepad is pictured at the left; TextEdit is at the right.

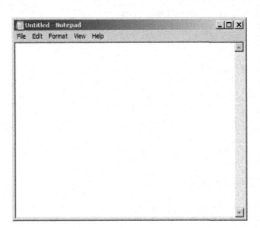 

3. Rehearse the script.

   ☐ using either Notepad or TextEdit (not Captivate), click the **File** menu

   ☐ click the **Page Setup** menu item

   ☐ from the **Orientation** area, click **Landscape**

   Note: In Notepad, Landscape is listed as the word "Landscape."
   In TextEdit, Landscape is the **second** tool (shown below).

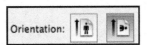

   ☐ click the **OK** button

   ☐ click the **File** menu

   ☐ click the **Page Setup** menu item

   ☐ click the **Portrait** orientation button

   ☐ click the **OK** button

   Hey, look at that! The script worked perfectly... no surprises. You are now ready to work the exact steps again. Only this time, you will record every click that you make. During the recording process, Captivate creates one screen capture each time that you click your mouse.

Student Activity: Review Recording Settings

1. Show Captivate's Preferences and set the Language and Audio Options.

   ☐ minimize or hide Notepad/TextEdit and return to Captivate (no Captivate projects should be open)

   ☐ if you are using Windows, choose **Edit > Preferences**; if you are using a Mac, choose **Adobe Captivate > Preferences**

   The Preferences dialog box opens. There are three main categories at the left: General Settings, Defaults, and Recording.

   ☐ select the **Recording** category

   ☐ from the **Generate Captions In** drop-down menu, ensure that **English** is selected

   Global Preferences: Recording: Settings

   Generate Captions In: | English ▼ |

   There are several languages available in the menu, including German, Italian, and Japanese. The language you select controls the text that appears in the Text Captions that are automatically created during the recording process.

   ☐ from the Audio Options area, deselect **Narration**, **System Audio**, **Actions in Real Time**, and **Keystrokes**

   ☐ from the Audio Options area, leave **Camera Sounds** selected

   The **Narration** option allows you to record a narrator at the same time that you record the lesson. Because you will not be using audio for the lesson you just rehearsed, you won't need this option. However, this feature could prove useful if you are relying on an SME to both record the lesson and provide the narration. Instead of creating the lesson and the narration on different days, both can be created at the same time. Nevertheless, I typically work with professional audio talent and import audio files into my Captivate projects later during production (you will work with audio on page 140). **System Audio** allows you to record any sounds made by your computer, such as audio associated with a video you are recording or the sound you hear when error messages appear in some applications.

   Audio Options: ☐ Narration | Audio Settings... |
   ☐ System Audio
   ☐ Actions in Real Time
   ☑ Camera Sounds
   ☐ Keystrokes
   ☐ Hear Keyboard Tap Sounds

   If you select **Actions in Real Time**, Captivate sets the slide timing for your project slides to match the time it took you to complete a process. If you wait 10 seconds from one click to the next, Captivate sets your slide timing to match. I typically do not use this feature. With **Camera Sounds** selected, you

hear a sound effect much like a camera shutter every time Captivate creates a screen capture. If you leave **Keystrokes** selected, Captivate creates an animation within your project that shows what you type, as you're typing—typos and all. I typically do not use this feature. Instead, I allow users to type text directly into my Captivate simulations using Text Entry Boxes. You will learn about Text Entry Boxes on page 183.

2. Set the Hide options.

   ☐ Windows users: from the Hide area, deselect **Recording Window**, **Task Icon**, and **System Tray Icon** (if necessary); Mac users, deselect **Recording Window** and **Dock Icon** (if necessary)

Hide: ☐ Recording Window	Hide: ☐ Recording Window
☐ Task Icon	☐ Dock Icon
☐ System Tray Icon	

   In the images above, the Windows options are shown at the left; the Mac options, at the right.

   If you had selected **Recording Window**, **Task Icon (Dock Icon)**, and **System Tray Icon**, you would hide all evidence of Captivate during the capture process. These items could get in the way if you were capturing your desktop and the Captivate application icon was on the screen. Because I tend to create software simulations within specific application windows, I typically leave these options deselected.

3. Ensure that new windows always appear in the Recording Area.

   ☐ from the Others area, ensure **Move New Windows Inside Recording Area** is selected

   The **Move New Windows Inside Recording Area** option could prove useful if a window tries to appear outside of the Recording Area. Captivate moves the window into the Recording Area for you. Without this feature, you would have to pause the movie, drag the window into the Recording Area, and continue. I typically enable this feature.

4. Enable Video recording.

   ☐ from the **Smoothen movements for** area, ensure both **Drag and Drop actions** and **Mouse Wheel Actions** are selected

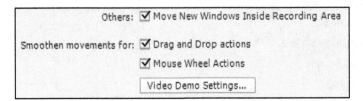

   These final two options deal with Video recordings, which you will learn about in "*Adobe Captivate 9: Beyond the Essentials.*"

5. Customize a recording key.

   ❑ from the **Recording** category at the left, select **Keys - (Global)**

   ❑ click in the **To Stop Recording** field and press the [**y**] key on your keyboard

   The letter [**y**] replaces the key that was in the field by default.

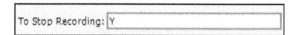

   If you were to move forward and record a lesson using Captivate, you would press [**y**] on your keyboard to end the recording process. You can customize the fields in this dialog box to suit your needs. For most people, the default keys work wonderfully.

6. Reset the default Recording Keys.

   ❑ still in the **Keys - (Global)** area, click the **Restore Defaults** button

   | Restore Defaults |

   Mac users: On my Mac, the default **To Stop Recording** shortcut keys [**Cmd**] [**Enter**] never works. I changed the keyboard shortcut to [**control**] [**e**] and things work perfectly every time.

   ❑ click the **OK** button

   When clicking the OK button, you might see the alert dialog box below.

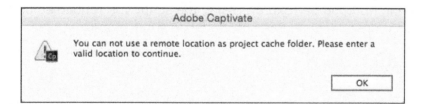

Project Cache is listed among the **General Settings** Preferences. Much like temporary Internet files created by web browsers as you surf the web, the Project Cache folder stores components of all of your projects until you click the **Clear Cache** button. The cached projects make the process of re-opening, saving, and working on projects faster than previous versions of Captivate. However, the Cache folder cannot be located on a remote location, such as a network or external drive. To resolve the issue presented in the dialog box above, select **General Settings** from the **Preferences** category list at the left. From the **Project Cache** area, click the **Browse** button. Open your Local Disk and either select a folder on the disk or create a new one. (I typically create a new folder called **CpCache** directly on the hard drive, but you can use any folder on the local disk). Once you've specified a local location for the cache, you should be able to click the **OK** button to close the Preferences dialog box.

Multimode Recordings

As first mentioned on page 40, there are multiple Automatic recording modes: Demonstration, Assessment Simulation, Training Simulation, and Custom. Each mode is covered during this module.

Demonstration mode is ideal if you want to show a quick software concept to someone, but you don't expect the person to follow along and actually perform the steps being demonstrated. When recording using Demonstration mode, Captivate automatically includes Text Captions (text bubbles that tell users what's happening on the screen), Highlight Boxes (colorful boxes), and a simulated mouse cursor that work together to grab the learner's attention.

Assessment simulations allow you to record and create interactive eLearning at one time. An Assessment includes Click Boxes (to make the lesson interactive) and Failure Captions (to help the user who clicks in the wrong place or performs the wrong step) by default. However, because an Assessment Simulation won't include Text Captions, an Assessment Simulation works best when teamed with a Demonstration. You've likely experienced this kind of eLearning: there's a "show me" lesson that demonstrates a concept; then there's an interactive "let me try" version of the same lesson that is interactive.

Training simulations are similar to Assessments. However, in addition to Click Boxes and Failure Captions being automatically added, you will also gain **Hint Captions** (captions that appear if the learner moves their mouse close to the Click Box but does not actually click anywhere).

Custom recordings can be set up to be a combination of the Demonstration, Assessment, and Training modes.

During the activities that follow, you will review Captivate's default preferences for recording Demonstrations, Assessment simulations, and Training simulations. Then you will use all three modes—at the same time—to record the process of changing the page orientation in Notepad or TextEdit (using the script you rehearsed on page 42).

Student Activity: Review Recording Modes

1. Ensure that Captivate is still running (no projects should be open).

2. Display Captivate's Preferences dialog box.

   ❏ if you are using Windows, choose **Edit > Preferences**; if you are using a Mac, choose **Adobe Captivate > Preferences**

3. Review the default settings for Demonstration mode.

   ❏ from the **Recording** categories at the left, select **Modes**

   Notice that there is a Mode drop-down menu at the right.

   ❏ from the **Mode** drop-down menu, choose **Demonstration**

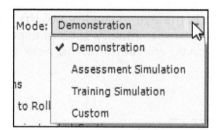

   ❏ from the bottom of the dialog box, click the **Restore Defaults** button

   It's possible that clicking the Restore Defaults button didn't do anything to the settings you see on your screen. However, clicking the button has reset the options to Captivate's original settings. Because I have no idea if you (or someone else) has changed the recording settings, it's a good idea to restore the defaults. At this point, the settings are back to what you would see after starting Captivate for the first time. After you have completed the lessons in this module, you can modify the recording settings.

   ❏ review the **Captions** area

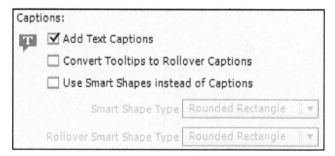

   In the Captions area, notice that **Add Text Captions** is selected by default. **Convert Tooltips to Rollover Captions** and **Use Smart Shapes instead of Captions** are both deselected. You will learn how to insert and work with Text Captions beginning on page 66. However, during the recording process, Captivate adds a bunch of Text Captions to your slide for you, which is, quite frankly, awesome. (When you see the automatic Text Captions, I dare you not to smile!) You will learn how to work with Smart Shapes on page 102 and Rollover Captions on page 128. Once you have mastered those Captivate

features, you can come back to this dialog box and experiment with what those two options do for your recording. For now, it's best to leave both options deselected.

❏ review the **Mouse** area

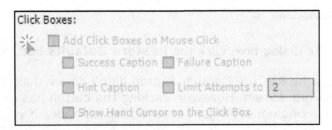

In the Mouse area, notice that **Show Mouse Location and Movement** and **Add Highlight Boxes on Click** are both selected by default. By including the Mouse Location, learners see a mouse move around the screen as they watch your demonstration. The mouse they see is actually mimicking where you pointed and clicked during the recording process. And by adding Highlight Boxes, learners see a colorful box that leads the eye to the area of the screen where the action is occurring. You will learn how to modify several aspects of the mouse pointer beginning on page 114; you will learn how to work with Highlight Boxes on page 119.

❏ review the **Click Boxes** area

In the Click Boxes area, notice that none of the options are selected... nor can you select them. Click Boxes add interactivity to your eLearning lessons. They're great, but because demonstrations are not interactive, you don't need Click Boxes. The other modes (which you will review next) rely heavily on Click Boxes. (You will learn how to add Click Boxes to a project manually beginning on page 179.)

❏ review the **Text Entry Boxes** area

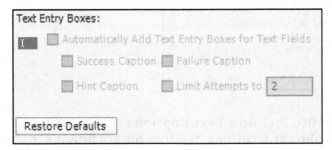

As with Click Boxes, Text Entry Boxes are deselected by default. Text Entry Boxes are also interactive and allow learners to type directly within a simulation. (You will learn how to add Text Entry Boxes to a project beginning on page 183.)

4. Review the default settings for Assessment Simulation mode.

   ☐ from the **Mode** drop-down menu, choose **Assessment Simulation**

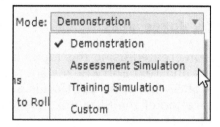

   ☐ from the bottom of the dialog box, click the **Restore Defaults** button

   ☐ review the **Captions** area

Because learners who take this lesson are expected to prove that they understand the demonstration they likely watched before opening the assessment, there isn't a need to include text captions. For that reason, the captions are disabled by default.

   ☐ review the **Mouse** area

Because this lesson is interactive, allowing Captivate to create an artificial mouse would be confusing to the learner. Both the Mouse and Highlight Box options are disabled by default.

   ☐ review the **Click Boxes** and **Text Entry Boxes** areas

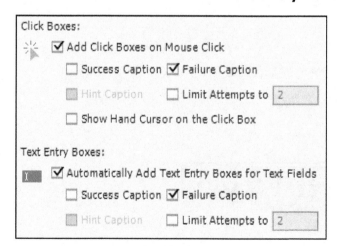

An Assessment Simulation is expected to be interactive. Both Click Boxes and Text Entry Boxes are selected by default. In addition, Failure Caption is enabled. If the learner clicks in the wrong place while moving through the lesson, the learner sees a correction via the Failure Caption.

5. Review the default settings for Training Simulation mode.

    ❑ from the **Mode** drop-down menu, choose **Training Simulation**

    ❑ from the bottom of the dialog box, click the **Restore Defaults** button

    ❑ review the **Captions** and **Mouse** areas

As with the Assessment Simulation, there is no need for captions, the mouse, or Highlight Boxes.

    ❑ review the **Click Boxes** and **Text Entry Boxes** areas

As with the Assessment Simulation, a lesson created using this mode is expected to be interactive. Both Click Boxes and Text Entry Boxes are selected by default (along with Failure Captions). Notice that **Hint Caption** is also selected. If the learner gets close to the location of the Click Box, the learner gets a hint about how to proceed. Hint Captions are great if your learner doesn't have strong mouse skills, tends to point at screen objects, but doesn't naturally click the mouse.

6. Close the Preferences dialog box by clicking the **OK** button.

Note to Mac Users: You're about to record screen actions. However, if you are using two monitors, it's possible that you won't see the red Captivate Recording Area shown on the next page. I've been able to get the recording area to appear by choosing **Apple > System Preferences > Displays > Arrangement** and selecting **Mirror Displays**. Although you won't be able to take advantage of having two monitors while recording screen actions using Captivate, you can turn off Mirror Displays once the recording process is complete.

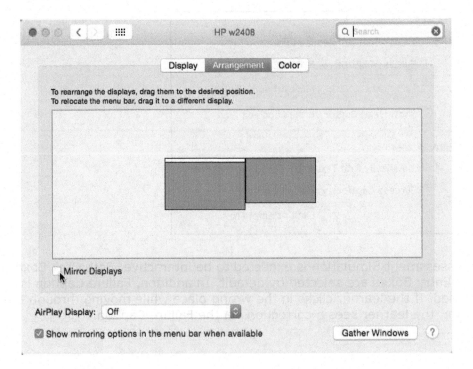

Student Activity: Record Using Multiple Modes

1. Ensure that Captivate is running (no projects should be open).

2. Ensure that Notepad or TextEdit is running (see page 42).

3. Display the Recording Area and control panel.

   ❏ from within Captivate, click the **New** tab on the Home screen

   ❏ double-click **Software Simulation** (or choose **File > Record new Software Simulation**)

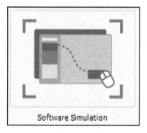

Software Simulation

Notice that there is a red box. Known as the Recording Area, this is the area of the screen that will be captured during the recording process. There is also a control panel containing Size and Recording Type controls.

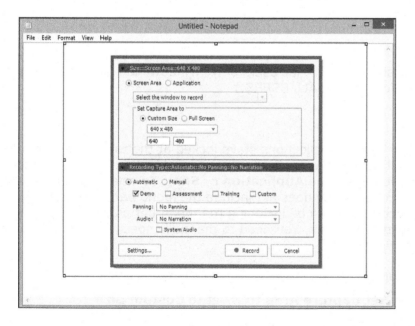

4. Specify what Captivate is supposed to record.

WINDOWS USERS:

☐ from the top of the control panel, select **Application**

☐ from the **Select the window to record** drop-down menu that appears, select **Untitled - Notepad**

On your screen, notice that the red Recording Area and Notepad occupy the same space. By specifying Notepad as the Application, Captivate's Recording Area is now focusing on Notepad

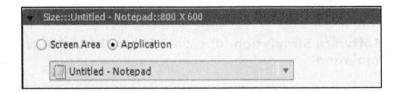

☐ from the **Snap to** area, select **Custom Size**

☐ select **800 x 600** from the drop-down menu

The Recording Area resizes to 800 x 600. And because you selected Application, the Notepad application also resizes to 800 x 600.

The next few steps are for Mac users only. Windows users, skip to **step 5** below. (Look for the text ALL USERS.)

MAC USERS:

The menu bar in your applications stays locked at the top of the screen (the menu does not float in the application's window like Windows applications). You won't typically use the **Application** or **Snap To** selections unless the process you are recording does not include the menu bar. During the following recording process, you will be including the menu bar as you change the Page Orientation within TextEdit. You need to manually specify a Screen Area for Captivate to record.

☐ from the top of the control panel, select **Screen Area**

☐ ensure the **Set Capture Area to** is set to **Custom Size**

☐ select **800 x 600** from the drop-down menu

❏ drag and resize the **TextEdit** window and red **Recording Area** as necessary until your screen looks similar to the image below (notice that the TextEdit menu bar is within the Recording Area)

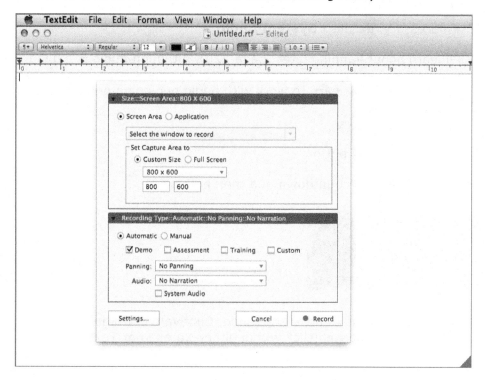

ALL USERS:

When recording, you should use the smallest Recording Size that works for you and the application or Screen Area that you are recording. Keep in mind that the smaller your Recording Area, the fewer megabytes your published video will be. The fewer the megabytes, the faster your learners can download and consume your eLearning content.

5. Select a Recording Mode.

❏ from the **Recording Type** area of the Control panel, select **Automatic**

With this option selected, every click of your mouse during the recording process creates a screen capture. In contrast, had you selected **Manual** mode, you would need to press a key on your keyboard (typically the [**print screen**] key for Windows users, [command] [F6] for Mac users) to capture the screen.

❏ select **Demo**, **Assessment**, and **Training** from the list of modes

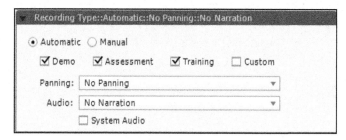

6. Disable Panning and Audio Narration.

❏ ensure that Panning is set to **No Panning** and that Audio is set to **No Narration**

❏ if necessary, deselect **System Audio**

You'll learn about Panning later (page 220). Although audio is a good thing in your eLearning, in my experience, it is best to create the audio later (during production). You will learn to work with audio beginning on page 139.

7. Record multiple modes.

❏ click the **Record** button

You see a 3-second countdown and then nothing.

While nothing seems to have happened, Captivate is waiting patiently for you to follow your script, and click within either Notepad or TextEdit.

❏ using your mouse, click the **File** menu within Notepad or TextEdit

❏ click the **Page Setup** menu item

❏ from the **Orientation** area, click **Landscape**

❏ click the **OK** button

❏ click the **File** menu

❏ click the **Page Setup** menu item

❏ click the **Portrait** orientation button and then click the **OK** button

8. Stop the recording.

❏ Windows users, press [**end**] on your keyboard; Mac users, press [**control**] [**e**] (or whatever stop recording shortcut you set up) on your keyboard

Once you stop the recording process, slides are created and three unsaved projects open in Captivate.

Note: If you can't get Captivate to stop recording via your keyboard shortcut, you can manually stop the recording process by clicking the Captivate icon in the **System Tray** (Windows users) or the **Dock** (Mac users).

9. Preview the demo.

❐ near the top of the Captivate window, notice that there are three tabs, one untitled project for each mode you selected prior to recording

untitled_demo1.cptx ×	untitled_assessment1.cptx ×	untitled_training1.cptx ×

❐ select the first tab (**untitled_demo1**)

❐ from the toolbar, click **Preview** and choose **Project**

As the preview plays, notice that the project contains text captions and Highlight Boxes. You will learn how to create captions from scratch as you move through the lessons in this book. If this is your first time automatically recording an eLearning project, there is a good chance you have just been blown away with the fact that Captivate added reasonable, usable text to your new lesson out of the box. *Very cool!*

Note to Mac users: If you didn't get any text captions during the recording process or you received an error message while trying to record, try this. Click the **Apple** menu and choose **System Preferences**. Select **Security & Privacy**. Select **Accessibility** and then, from the **Allow the apps below to control your computer** area, select **Adobe Captivate.app**. Close the window and then try recording again.

10. When the preview is finished, close the preview by pressing the [**Esc**] key on your keyboard.

11. Close the demo project (there is no need to save it).

Two projects should still be open: **untitled_assessment** and **untitled_training**.

Preview Confidence Check

1. Preview the **untitled_assessment** project. As you do, notice that using this mode has created an interactive simulation. You can click where you were supposed to click to move to the next slide and continue the lesson. Click anywhere else on the screen to see a Failure Caption.

2. When finished with the **untitled_assessment** project, close it without saving it.

3. Preview the **untitled_training** project. As you do, notice that using this lesson is nearly identical to the assessment lesson you just closed. However, when you move your mouse close to the area of the screen where you are supposed to click, you see the Hint Captions.

You've got to admit that this is awesome stuff... three modes, three projects... and all it took you was a few clicks here and there.

4. When finished with the **untitled_training** project, close it without saving it.

Custom Recordings

You have now learned how to record three kinds of eLearning lessons with Adobe Captivate: Demonstrations, Assessment Simulations, and Training Simulations. Between demonstrations and simulations, which type of lesson results is the most effective learning experience for your users? There is no clear-cut answer.

Demonstrations are relatively quick and easy to create (you just did). However, demonstrations do not allow for learner interaction. When learners watch a demonstration rather than participate in an interactive simulation, the potential for learning is reduced. The Text Captions that are automatically created by Captivate are great, but they are written in the imperative, or command, form. For instance, a typical Text Caption created by Captivate is likely to say something like "Select the File Menu." Upon reading that instruction, a learner is likely to take the caption's instructions literally and attempt to select the File menu. Unfortunately, at the same time that the learner is trying to interact with the demonstration, a mouse pointer that Captivate created when the lesson was recorded is likely moving around the screen. In this case, you're going to end up with one confused and possibly frustrated learner.

Simulations are perfect for assessing what a learner has absorbed during a demonstration. However, because Simulations do not add any Text Captions by default, there are no instructions telling learners what to do. Learners either perform the required steps or click incorrectly somewhere on the screen and see a Failure Caption. Some people consider this kind of approach to eLearning to be a bit harsh because the learner is often experiencing negative feedback with no guidance.

Many Captivate developers create both a Demonstration and a Simulation. That's all well and good until you remember that it could take several hours to produce the lessons. If you elect to produce both a Demonstration and an Assessment, you are essentially making twice the work for yourself.

Demonstration or Simulation: Which Mode is Best?

Instead of creating a Demonstration and a Simulation, I recommend you record a custom, or hybrid, lesson that incorporates the best of the Demonstration, Assessment, and Training modes.

When you are finished recording the custom lesson, the result is a lesson that bridges the gap between a Demonstration and an Assessment/Simulation lesson.

Student Activity: Record a Custom Simulation

1. Set the Preferences for the simulation you are about to record.

   ❑ Windows users, choose **Edit > Preferences**;
   Mac users, choose **Adobe Captivate > Preferences**

   ❑ from the **Recording** category, select **Modes**

   ❑ from the Mode drop-down menu, select **Custom**

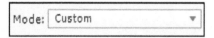

   ❑ click the **Restore Defaults** button at the bottom of the dialog box

   ❑ from the Captions area, select **Add Text Captions**

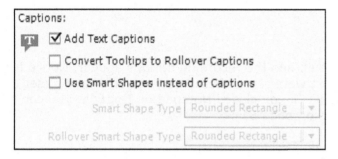

   ❑ from the Click Boxes area, select **Add Click Boxes on Mouse Click** and **Failure Caption**

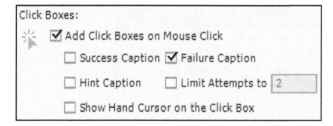

   By now you should be somewhat comfortable with the available options in this dialog box. You have selected **Add Text Captions** so that the Text Captions are created for you (like you saw with a Demonstration). *Nice.* And because the captions are written in the imperative, you may be able to use them in the new lesson with little editing. *Nicer.* Everything else has been left deselected except for **Click Boxes** and **Failure Caption** (like the simulation modes). These two settings result in a highly interactive simulation out of the box. *Nicest!*

   ❑ click the **OK** button

2. Record the custom simulation.

☐ from within Captivate, click the **New** tab on the Home screen

☐ double-click **Software Simulation** (or choose **File > Record new Software Simulation**)

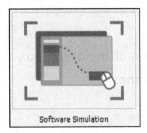

Captivate once again hides, and the recording options appear. Notice that the settings you specified last were remembered so you don't have to set the Screen Area options again (if you closed Notepad or TextEdit, you can review the Screen Area settings on page 51).

3. Record the Custom simulation.

☐ from the **Recording Type** area, select **Custom**

☐ deselect the other modes

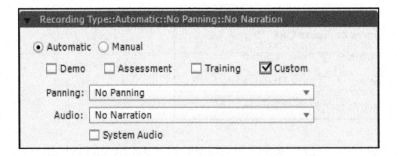

☐ click the **Record** button and, once the Countdown goes away, use your mouse to click the **File** menu within Notepad or TextEdit

☐ click the **Page Setup** menu item

☐ from the **Orientation** area, click **Landscape**

☐ click the **OK** button

☐ click the **File** menu

☐ click the **Page Setup** menu item

☐ click the **Portrait** orientation button

☐ click the **OK** button

4. Stop the recording process.

5. Preview the project.

   As you move through the lesson, notice that the Text Captions are written in the imperative to encourage interactivity. There may be one or two captions you need to edit (some of the buttons are likely mislabeled, especially on the Mac side). Nevertheless, much of the caption-writing work is done.

   Also notice that there are Click Boxes (hot spots) that make this lesson 100 percent interactive.

6. When finished previewing the lesson, close the preview.

7. Close the project (there is no need to save it).

Recording Confidence Check

Record a lesson using caption written in a language other than English:

1. Display the Preferences dialog box (Edit menu for Windows users; Adobe Captivate menu for Mac users).

2. From the categories at the left, select **Recording**.

3. From the **Generate Captions In** drop-down menu, choose any language.

Global Preferences: Recording: Settings

Generate Captions In: | Italian ▼

Note: If you do not have the Asian fonts installed on your computer, you might want to select a language other than the Asian languages. Without the Asian fonts, you'll see white boxes instead of letters in the resulting Text Captions.

4. Create another Software Simulation with Notepad or TextEdit that uses the Custom mode. (When you record the simulation, run through the same script you have used throughout this module).

5. Stop the recording process and preview the project.

   Notice that the Text Captions are using the language you specified in the **Generate Captions In** drop-down menu.

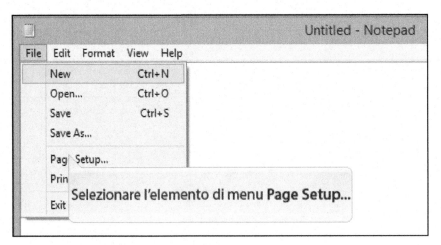

Untitled - Notepad

| File | Edit | Format | View | Help |

New	Ctrl+N
Open...	Ctrl+O
Save	Ctrl+S
Save As...
Pag Setup...
Prin
Exit

Selezionare l'elemento di menu **Page Setup...**

6. Close the project (there is no need to save it when prompted).

7. Display the **Preferences** dialog box again and set the Recording language back to English.

8. Close Notepad/TextEdit (there is no need to save if prompted).

Panning

Captivate's Panning feature is useful when you want to record something on your computer that is outside of the red Recording Area. If you enable Panning prior to recording and use Captivate's Automatic mode, clicking outside of the Recording Area forces Captivate to move the Recording Area and includes the area you clicked. You can also use Manual Panning where you drag the Recording Area to the area of the screen you would like to record.

Student Activity: Record a Demonstration that Pans

1. Start a web browser and navigate to **www.disney.com**.

2. Switch to Captivate and create a new Software Simulation.

3. Select a screen area to record instead of a specific application.

   ❑ from the top of the control panel, select **Screen Area**

4. Specify a recording size.

   ❑ from the Set Capture Area to area, select **Custom Size**

   ❑ from the next drop-down menu, select **640 x 480**

5. Drag the red recording box to the **upper left** of the browser window.

6. Resize the browser window so it's about 30 percent larger than the red Recording Area.

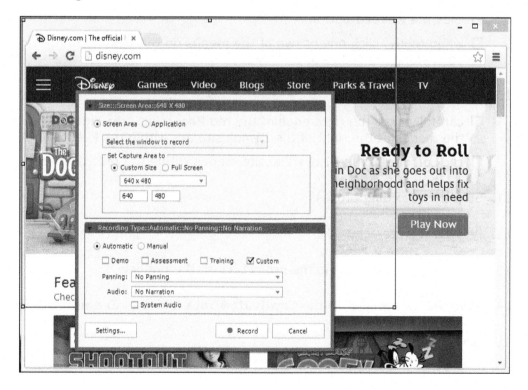

Because you selected Screen Area instead of Application, the red Recording Area stays sized to 640 x 480 and does not get larger as you resize the browser window.

More important, there are menus on the Disney site that are not within the red recording area (the TV menu in the image above, for example). If you record now and click any of the menus outside of the recording area, none of those actions will be recorded. This is a perfect place to use the Panning feature.

7. Select a Recording Mode.

   ❏ from the Recording Type area of the Control panel, ensure **Automatic** is selected

   ❏ from the list of modes, select **Demo** and then **deselect** the other modes

8. Enable Panning.

   ❏ from the **Panning** drop-down menu, choose **Manual Panning**

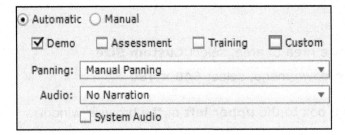

9. Record the Demo.

   ❏ click the **Record** button

   ❏ when ready, click one or two of the menus on the Disney.com navigation bar (within the red Recording Area)

10. Manually pan.

   ❏ carefully drag the right edge of the red Recording Area **right** so some of the menus at the right of the Disney site are within the Recording Area

   ❏ click on one of the Disney website menus within the recording area

11. Stop the recording process.

12. Preview the project.

13. When finished previewing the project, close the preview.

14. Save the new project to the **Captivate9Data** folder as **ExampleOfPanning**.

15. Close the project.

Manual Recordings

If you've stepped through all of the activities in this module, you've now used every recording option in Captivate except two—Manual mode and Video mode (Video Mode is covered in *Adobe Captivate 9: Beyond the Essentials*). In most instances, recording screen actions using Captivate's Automatic Recording type gets the job done for you. However, you will come across some applications where attempting to record automatically does not work (some applications won't get along with Captivate and prove difficult to record). This is a perfect opportunity to use Captivate's Manual recording type.

> **Note:** If you are running a screen capture utility (such as SnagIt), disable or close it prior to trying to record manually with Captivate. If a competing screen capture application is running, that program will grab screen captures instead of Captivate.

Student Activity: Manually Record the Screen

1. Ensure that Captivate is still running (no projects should be open).

2. Rehearse the lesson you are going to record.

   ❏ return to the Disney website: **www.disney.com**

   ❏ point, but don't click on some of the links on the Disney site

   You'd like to capture the process of pointing to site objects, but recording the action with Captivate is going to be difficult because it takes mouse clicks to create screen captures.

3. Display the recording control panel.

   ❏ return to Captivate and create a new **Software Simulation**

4. Select the Disney site as the Application to record.

   ❏ from the top of the control panel, select **Application**

   ❏ from the Select window drop-down menu, choose the Disney site

   ❏ from the Snap to area, select **Custom Size**

   ❏ from the next drop-down menu, choose **640 x 480** (if necessary)

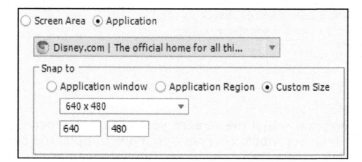

5. Select the Manual Recording Type.

   ❑ from the Recording Type area of the Control panel, select **Manual**

   ❑ change the Panning to **No Panning**

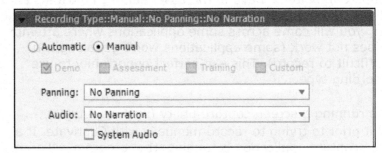

6. Record the Manual Demo.

   ❑ click the **Record** button

   Unlike the other modes, no screen capture is created for you. You'll need to create every screen capture on your own.

   ❑ Windows users, press [**Print Screen**] on your keyboard; Mac users, press [**Command**] [**F6**]

   ❑ point to one of the links on the navigation bar

   ❑ Windows users, press [**Print Screen**] on your keyboard; Mac users, press [**Command**] [**F6**]

   ❑ point to another one of the links on the navigation bar

   ❑ Windows users, press [**Print Screen**] on your keyboard; Mac users, press [**Command**] [**F6**]

   Note: Mac users may find it tough, if not impossible, to use the function keys to create manual shots because those keys might activate special features (those special features are printed on each key). You can disable the special features by displaying the Mac's **System Preferences** (via the Apple menu) and selecting **Keyboard**. On the **Keyboard** tab, select **Use all F1, F2, etc. keys as standard function keys**. Alternatively, you can display the **Keys - Global** Preference within Captivate and change the Manual Recording Key.

   ☑ Use all F1, F2, etc. keys as standard function keys
   When this option is selected, press the Fn key to use the special features printed on each key.

7. Stop the recording.

8. Preview the project, and notice that the screens you captured appear. But this is a bare-bones recording. You would now need to move through the project and add required project assets that recording in the Automatic mode would normally have included (Text Captions, Highlight Boxes, etc.).

9. Close the project (there is no need to save it).

iCONLOGiC

"Skills and Drills" Learning

Module 4: Captions, Styles, and Timing

In This Module You Will Learn About:

And You Will Learn To:

Text Captions

Text Captions are typically used to explain a concept being shown onscreen. You can have multiple text captions on the same slide, and you can control how the captions look (to a limited degree), where they appear on the slide, and when they appear (via the Timeline or the Properties Inspector).

Student Activity: Insert and Edit Text Captions

1. Using Adobe Captivate, open the **CaptionMe** project from the **Captivate9Data** folder.

2. Reset the Classic workspace.

   ❐ choose **Window > Workspace > Reset Classic**

   By resetting the Classic workspace, any inspectors or toolbars that you might have opened during previous lessons in this book are put away, and your Captivate window should be clutter-free.

3. Preview the lesson.

   ❐ choose **Preview > Project**

   This project is a demonstration that was recorded using Captivate's Demonstration mode (you learned how to create a software demonstration beginning on page 46). The lesson demonstrates the process of creating a new folder on an older version of Windows. It's a perfectly fine demonstration, but there are no Text Captions telling the learner what's about to happen or why. During the next several activities, you will learn how to add Text Captions to several slides. You will also learn how to control the appearance of the captions and when they appear on the slide.

4. Close the Preview.

5. Show Captivate's Preferences.

   ❐ Windows users, choose **Edit > Preferences**; Mac users, choose **Adobe Captivate > Preferences**

6. Restore the timing and style defaults used for inserted objects.

   ❐ from the top of the **Category** list at the left, select **Defaults**

   ❐ from the **Object Defaults** area, click the **Restore All** button

Restore Selected	Restore All

   By clicking the Restore All button, any objects you insert into your Captivate projects (such as Text Captions) use the default timing and appearance specified by Adobe when Captivate was first installed on your computer. You will learn how to change the timing and style used by objects as you move through lessons in this book.

   ❐ click the **OK** button

7. Insert a Text Caption.

   ❏ on the **Filmstrip**, select slide **1**

   ❏ on the toolbar, click **Text** and choose **Text Caption**

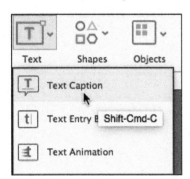

The new Text Caption appears in the middle of the slide.

   ❏ replace the text in the caption with **Watch as the File menu is selected**

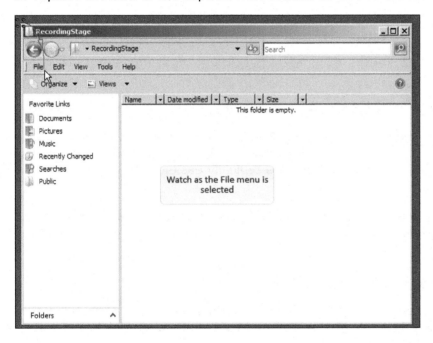

8. Deselect the caption.

   ❏ click above or below the Text Caption

   With the caption deselected, you cannot edit the text within the caption, nor can you change the appearance of the caption or its slide location.

9. Use the Properties Inspector to change the Caption type for a selected Text Caption.

   ❏ on slide **1, select the Text Caption**

   ❏ at the far right of the Captivate window, click **Properties**

Because you selected the text caption on the slide, the Properties Inspector is displaying the properties of the selected caption.

☐ on the **Properties Inspector**, locate the **Caption Type** drop-down menu

☐ from the **Caption Type** drop-down menu, choose **HaloGreen**

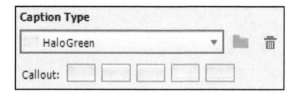

10. Resize a Text Caption.

☐ with the Text Caption still selected, position your mouse pointer on one of the Text Caption's resizing handles (the squares)

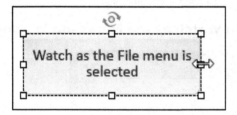

☐ drag the resizing handle until the size of the Text Caption looks good to you

Although the exact size of any Text Caption is always up to you, consider making your Text Captions **narrow** and **tall** as opposed to wide and short. Narrow and tall text captions are typically easier to read than wide and short captions.

Note: As you work with more of the Caption Types, you'll discover that some captions can be made only so small, while other types have fewer limitations on size.

11. Reposition a Text Caption on a slide.

☐ with the Text Caption still selected, drag the middle of the caption toward the **top left** side of the slide and position it so your slide looks similar to the picture below

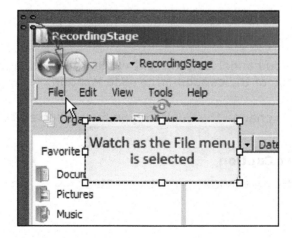

Student Activity: Modify Text Caption Properties

1. Ensure that the **CaptionMe** project is still open.

2. Change the Caption type.

   ❑ on slide **1**, select the Text Caption (if necessary)

   ❑ on the **Properties Inspector**, locate the **Caption Type** drop-down menu

   ❑ from the **Caption Type** drop-down menu, choose **Adobe Red**

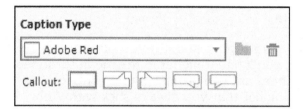

   Hey! Did the size of that pesky Text Caption change when you changed the Caption type? There's a very good chance that it did. Why? Captivate's **Autosize Captions** feature is enabled by default. Although the feature might seem like a good thing, I've found that it often forces me to do extra work because Text Captions that I've already resized *magically* resize when I change the way they look (like you just did) or when I edit the text.

3. Disable the Autosize Captions option.

   ❑ Windows users, choose **Edit > Preferences**; Mac users, choose **Adobe Captivate > Preferences**

   ❑ from the top of the Category list at the left, select **Defaults**

   ❑ from the **General** area at the bottom of the dialog box, deselect **Autosize Captions**

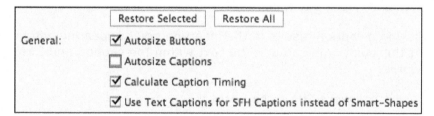

   ❑ click the **OK** button

   There won't be any visible change to the Text Caption on your slide. You'll see the results of disabling Autosize Captions next.

4. Resize the Text Caption again... this time, make it significantly larger.

5. Use the Properties Inspector to change the Caption Type to **Frosted**.

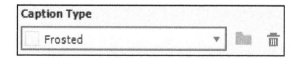

Although the general appearance of the Text Caption certainly changes, there are no changes to the size of the Text Caption. Is that a good thing or a bad thing? I guess it depends on your perspective. Certainly, if you want Captivate to resize your Text Captions moving forward, turn the Autosize Captions option back on. I always leave the option deselected.

6. Change the character formatting for the caption text.

   ❒ ensure the Text Caption on slide 1 is still selected

   ❒ on the Properties Inspector, locate the **Character** area

   ❒ change the font to **Verdana**

   Note: When selecting Verdana, you won't find it if you scroll too deep down the Font menu. Instead, you'll find it higher in the menu (grouped among the Web Safe fonts). There are two groups of fonts in Captivate: **Web Safe** and **System**. I'd suggest that you always stick with Web Safe fonts. While there are just a few Web Safe fonts from which to choose, most computers (Mac and Windows) have the Web Safe Fonts installed. If you select Web Safe fonts, there's a better chance that you won't run into missing font issues when learners access your eLearning content.

   ❒ change the size to **15 pt**

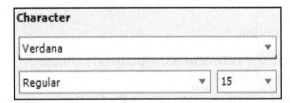

7. Change the appearance of a single word.

   ❒ double-click inside the text caption

   Double-clicking a caption results in the insertion point appearing within the caption. At this point, you can edit the text within the caption and format selected words.

   ❒ double-click the word **File** to highlight it

   ❒ from the **Character** area on the Properties Inspector, select the **Bold** command

   $$\boxed{\mathbf{B} \quad I \quad \underline{U} \quad T^2 \quad T_2}$$

   The Text Caption should look similar to the image below.

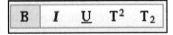

   Watch as the **File** menu is selected

Confidence Check

1. Ensure that the CaptionMe project is still open.

2. On slide **1**, change the Caption type for the Text Caption to **Adobe Blue**. (Need help? See page 69.)

3. Go to slide **3**.

4. Insert a Text Caption with the words **Watch as the New command is selected**.

    Notice that the formatting of the new Text Caption does not match the appearance of your first Text Caption. No worries... you'll learn how to ensure consistent formatting of slide objects very soon. For now, you're only concerned with knowing how to insert a Text Caption, not necessarily making it look good.

5. Go to slide **4** and insert a new Text Caption that says **Watch as the Folder command is selected**.

6. Go to slide **6** and insert a new Text Caption that says **Watch as the new Folder is selected**

7. Save and then close the project.

Caption Styles

During the activity that began on page 66, you learned how to insert a Text Caption and then how to change its formatting. Did you notice that every time you inserted a Text Caption, the appearance of the caption reverted to a specific Caption type, font, and font size? Although it is easy enough to change the appearance of the caption, you will quickly tire of the effort required to change every caption. Instead, you can alter the way Text Captions appear in this project via Caption Styles. Once you set up the appearance of the Caption Style, all new captions take on the attributes of the style and save you from extensive manual formatting.

Student Activity: Edit the Default Caption Style

1. Using Captivate, open **StyleMe** from the **Captivate9Data** folder.

2. Go from slide to slide and notice that most of the slides in this project contain a Text Caption. The appearance of each Text Caption is identical (HaloBlue, Calibri, 16 pt).

3. Override a style.

   ❏ go to slide **3** and select the Text Caption

   ❏ using the **Properties Inspector**, change the **Caption Type** to **HaloGreen**

   ❏ from the Character area, change the font to **Verdana** and the size to **15**

   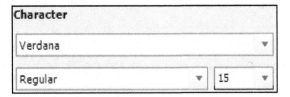

   The three changes you made to the caption have had an obvious effect on the selected Text Caption on slide 3. But what about the Text Captions on the other slides?

4. Explore the other slides.

   ❏ go from slide to slide and notice that none of the other Text Captions have taken on the appearance of the Text Caption on slide 3

5. Observe an Object Style override.

   ❏ return to slide **3** and select the Text Caption that you just formatted

   ❏ at the top of the **Properties Inspector**, locate the **Style Name** area

   A style named **[Default Caption Style]** is selected in the drop-down menu, indicating that it's the style being used by the selected Text Caption. In fact, all of the Text Captions in the StyleMe project are using the Default Caption

Style, which explains the reason that the appearance of every Text Caption in the project is consistent.

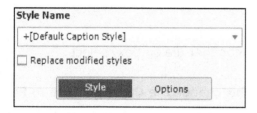

Okay, okay, you caught me. I said above that every Text Caption in the project is using the [Default Caption Style]. I should have stated that *most of the captions are following the [Default Caption Style]*. In fact, the Text Caption on slide 3 is following only a portion of the formatting specified in the style. How can you tell? Take a look at the name of the style in the Style drop-down menu. There's a plus sign to the left of the style's name.

The plus sign indicates that something about the way the caption has been formatted doesn't match the intent of the style. Unfortunately, there's no way to tell exactly what the formatting issue is, but the plus sign is a handy way to quickly determine that the formatting is different in some way.

I'm betting that you don't have a huge staff to support your eLearning development efforts. I'm also pretty sure that you don't have hours to waste on manual labor. If you use the Properties Inspector to format every object on every slide, you'll find yourself formatting and formatting and formatting. And when you're done, you'll format some more. I don't want to even think about how much extra work you will have to deal with if you want (or your boss wants) to update the appearance of the captions throughout the project. For that reason, I discourage you from using the Properties Inspector to change the way any object looks. You'll find it much more efficient to change the way things look via the Object Style Manager (you'll play with that soon). Instead, use the Properties Inspector to change the way objects behave (Timing, Actions, etc.). Those kinds of properties are not controlled by an Object Style.

6. Reset a style.

   ❑ with the Text Caption on slide 3 still selected, click the menu to the right of **Style Name** and choose **Reset Style**

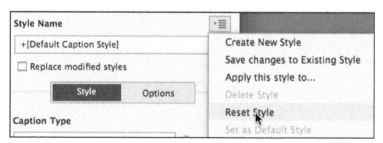

The plus sign goes away, and the selected Text Caption is once again following the properties of the Default Caption Style (HaloBlue, Calibri, 16 pt).

7. Edit the Default Caption Style.

❏ choose **Edit > Object Style Manager**

The Object Style Manager opens.

❏ from the top of the Object Style Manager dialog box, select **[Default Caption Style]**

❏ from the **Caption** area at the right, change the **Caption Type** to **Frosted**

❏ from the **Text Format** area, change the Family to **Verdana**

❏ change the Size to **15**

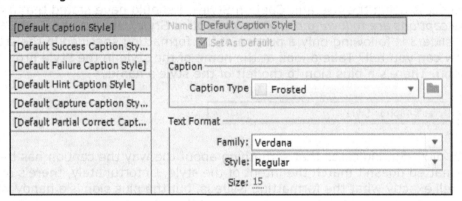

❏ click the **OK** button

Every caption in the project is now using the new Caption type and Text formatting. Don't you love object styles? Make a few edits in one place (the Object Style Manager), and potentially hundreds of slide objects are updated instantly. *Cool!*

8. Save your work.

Callouts

You learned how to apply a Caption type on page 69. While Caption types define the general look of the caption (HaloGreen, Adobe Blue, etc.), Callouts give a Text Caption direction. Most Caption Types include up to five Callouts that point to different areas of the slide. While Caption types are part of an Object Style (page 72), Callouts are options you manually apply to a selected object, one object at a time.

Student Activity: Change a Callout Used by a Text Caption

1. Ensure that the **StyleMe** project is still open.

2. Change the Callout used on a Text Caption.

    ☐ go to slide **1**

    The Callout being used on the Text Caption is a simple rectangle.

    ☐ select the **Text Caption**

    ☐ on the Properties Inspector, select the third Callout

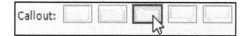

The caption now points up and to the left. The arrow helps guide the learner's eye toward the area of the screen where the mouse action is occurring.

Confidence Check

1. Move the Text Caption up and to the left a bit until the position is similar to the image below.

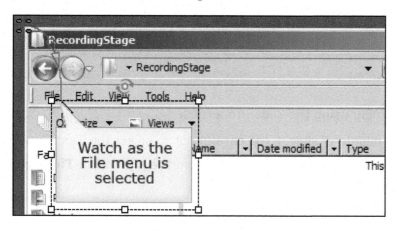

2. Go through the remaining slides and apply the third Callout to the rest of the captions.

3. Position (drag) each of the captions on the slides where you think appropriate.

4. Save and close the project.

The Timeline

The Timeline is at the bottom of the Captivate window. Each slide has a unique Timeline. You can use the Timeline to control the timing of any slide object. For instance, using the Timeline, you can force the captions to appear on the slide at the same time, or you can force one caption to appear as another goes away. The Timeline consists of the following features: Object Bars, a Header, a Playhead, and Playback Controls. The objects on a project slide are displayed as stacked bars on the left side of the Timeline. The Header at the top of the Timeline indicates time in seconds (and parts of seconds). The Playhead shows the point in time in which the slide is being viewed.

Student Activity: Control Slide and Object Timing

1. Using Captivate, open **TimeMe** from the **Captivate9Data** folder.

2. Display the Timeline.

   ☐ at the bottom of the Captivate window, click **Timeline**

3. Use the Timeline to extend the slide duration to eight seconds.

   ☐ on the Timeline, position your mouse pointer on the far right edge of the **Slide 1** object bar (until your mouse pointer looks like a double-headed arrow)

   ☐ drag the **right edge** of the object to the **right** until you get to **00:08** seconds on the Timeline (the word **End** should line up with the 00:08 mark on the Timeline)

   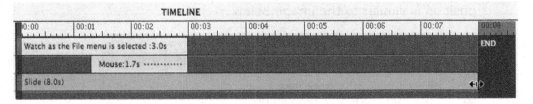

4. Extend slide timing using the slide Properties.

   ☐ click in the middle of slide 1 (be careful not to select the Text Caption)

   ☐ open the **Properties Inspector** and, from the right, click **Timing** to open the **Timing Inspector**

   ☐ change the **Slide Duration** to **10** sec

   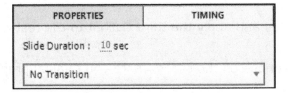

On the Timeline, notice that changing the Display Time on the Properties Inspector is exactly the same thing as dragging the right edge of the slide object to 10 seconds on the Timeline.

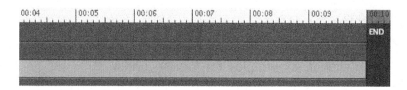

5. Use the Timeline to extend the display time for a Text Caption.

    ❑ on the **Timeline**, select the object **"Watch as the File menu is selected"**

    This object represents the **Watch as the File menu is selected** Text Caption on the slide.

    ❑ on the **Timeline**, drag the **right edge** of the **"Watch as the File menu is selected"** object **right** until the object is stretched to **00:04** seconds

6. Use the Timeline to change the timing for the mouse.

    ❑ still working on slide 1, select the **Mouse** object on the Timeline

    This object represents the mouse pointer on the slide.

    ❑ drag the middle of the **Mouse object** right until its left edge lines up with **00:04** on the Timeline

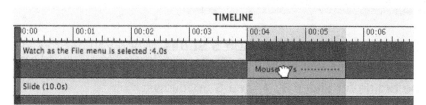

Confidence Check

1. Still working in the TimeMe project, change the Slide Duration for slide **1** to **5.7** seconds. (Need help? See page 76.)

2. Preview the first five slides.

   The Text Caption on slide **1** should play for four seconds. After the Text Caption disappears from the slide, the mouse pointer should move from the upper left of the slide to the slide's File menu. Once the action on slide **1** finishes, you're off to slide **2**.

   While on slide **2**, notice that it takes too much time for the click to actually occur—the timing needs work.

3. Close the preview and go to slide **2**. On the Timeline, select the **Mouse** object and, using the **Timing Inspector**, change the **Appear After** to **0 sec**.

4. From the **Timing** area, change the **Display For Specific Time** to **0.5 sec**

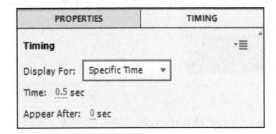

5. On the Timeline, change the Slide Duration to **0.5** sec.

6. Starting with slide **1**, preview the **Next 5 Slides**. When you get to slide **2**, the timing of the mouse click should be better.

7. Change the timing for slides **3**, **4**, and **6** as follows:

   Text Captions: Appear After **0 sec**; Display For Specific Time: **4 sec**

   Mouse objects: Appear After **4 sec**; Display For Specific Time: **1.7 sec**

   Slide Duration: **5.7 sec**

8. Change the timing for slide **5** as follows:

   Mouse object Appears After: **0 sec**; Displays For Specific Time: **0.5 sec**

   Slide Duration: **0.5 sec** (**Note:** If you have trouble using the Properties Inspector to change the Slide Duration to 0.5, use the Timeline.)

9. Preview the project. The timing between slides and objects should be smooth. When finished, close the preview, save, and close the project.

Student Activity: Check Spelling

1. Open **SpellMeAlignMe** from the **Captivate9Data** folder.

   This is pretty much the same project you've been working on since the beginning of this module. To save you a little work, I've added an introduction slide that explains the upcoming lesson. I timed the Text Captions so that each one plays for five seconds and appears on the slide one after the other.

2. Disable Calculate Caption Timing.

   ❑ Windows users, choose **Edit > Preferences**;
   Mac user, choose **Adobe Captivate > Preferences**

   ❑ from the top of the dialog box, select **Defaults**

   ❑ from the **General** area, deselect **Calculate Caption Timing**

   ☐ Autosize Captions
   ☐ Calculate Caption Timing

   Depending on how you look at the world, the Calculate Caption Timing feature is one of those "glass half empty, half full" kind of commands. With the option selected, Captivate automatically calculates how long a caption stays on a slide based on the number of characters in the caption. *That's a glass half-full kind of thing—you don't have to worry about the timing.*

   However, if you select a specific display time (as you have done with the captions in this project) and then change a caption's content, you would inadvertently reset your specified time to Captivate's calculated caption timing. *That's a glass half-empty kind of thing—you'll have to reset the timing via the Timeline or through the Text Caption's properties.* I always disable Calculate Caption Timing.

   ❑ click the **OK** button

3. On slide **1**, notice that there are typos in the Text Captions (from misspelled words to double words). No worries, you'll be fixing each of the typos during the Check Spelling activity that follows.

4. Spell check the project.

   ❑ choose **Project > Check Spelling**

   The Check Spelling dialog box opens. The first word that is flagged as Not In Dictionary is the word **foolders**. It should be replaced with the word **folders**.

❏ ensure that **folders** is selected in the **Suggestions** area

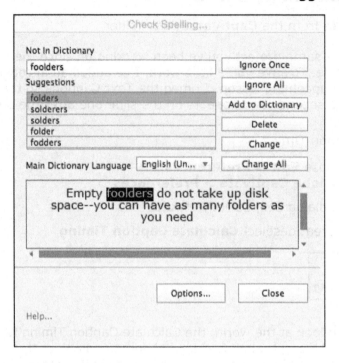

❏ click the **Change** button

The next error is the double word "you."

❏ click the **Delete** button

The word "demmonstration" is flagged as Not In Dictionary.

❏ select **demonstration** from the list of Suggestions and then click the **Change** button

The double word "is" is flagged.

❏ click the **Delete** button

The word "seelected" is flagged as Not In Dictionary.

❏ select **selected** from the list of Suggestions and then click the **Change** button

Once the Spell Check is complete, you are alerted to the total number of corrections made.

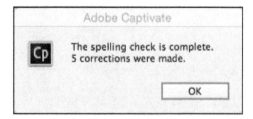

❏ click the **OK** button

Student Activity: Align Slide Objects

1. Ensure that the **SpellMeAlignMe** project is still open.

2. Hide an object.

   ☐ go to slide **1**

   There are four Text Captions on the slide. You'll soon use Captivate's alignment features to line up three of the four captions. One of the captions is in the way. Rather than drag it out of the way, only to have to drag it back, it is more efficient to temporarily hide it.

   ☐ if necessary, display the **Timeline** (you learned how to display the Timeline on page 76)

   ☐ on the left side of the Timeline, click the first circle just beneath the eyeball

   The circle becomes a red x. The "**During this demonstration**" caption disappears from the slide (although it's still visible on the Timeline).

   | 0:00 | 00:01 | 00:02 | 00:03 | 00:04 |
   | During this demonstration you will see how to create a new folder :5. |

   With the top-most caption hidden, you can easily see the three remaining captions. Even though the caption is hidden from view, it will still preview and publish.

3. Select multiple captions.

   ☐ click one time on the caption containing "New folders can be..."

   ☐ press and hold the [**shift**] key on your keyboard

   ☐ click one time on the caption containing "You can give your folder..."

   ☐ keep the [**shift**] key down on your keyboard

   ☐ click one time on the caption containing "Empty folders do not take..."

   ☐ release the [**shift**] key

   All three captions should be selected.

4. Left-align the selected captions.

   ☐ choose **Modify > Align > Align Left**

   The selected objects aligned to the left.

   ☐ choose **Modify > Align > Distribute Vertically**

   The captions are now lined up with the first caption you selected (objects with white handles serve as anchors, and other selected objects move to the anchors when you align objects). In addition, the vertical space between the selected captions is evenly spaced.

Confidence Check

1. Ensure that the **SpellMeAlignMe** project is still open.

2. Ensure you are on slide **1**, and choose **Preview > Next 5 slides**.

3. As slide **1** plays, notice that the timing of the Text Captions is pretty good. But don't you think it would be better if the three Text Captions (after the first one) stayed around for the duration of the slide? Sure you do!

4. Close the preview and return to slide **1**.

5. Select all three of the visible Text Captions on slide **1** (the first Text Caption should still be hidden).

6. Choose **Modify > Show for the rest of the slide**.

   On the Timeline, notice that the selected objects have stretched to the end of the slide.

7. Preview the first five slides.

   Notice that after the first Text Caption goes away, the remaining captions show for the rest of the slide.

8. Show the hidden Caption.

9. Close the preview.

10. Save and close the project.

iCONLOGiC

"Skills and Drills" Learning

Module 5: Images and Smart Shapes

In This Module You Will Learn About:

And You Will Learn To:

Images

Captivate lets you import several graphic formats onto a slide including, but not limited to, native **Photoshop** documents (PSDs), **BMPs** (Windows Bitmap), **GIFs** (Graphics Interchange Format), **JPG** or **JPEG** (Joint Photographic Expert Group), **ICOs** (icons), **WMFs** (MetaFiles), **EMFs** (Enhanced MetaFiles), **PNGs** (Portable Network Graphics), and **POTs** (PowerPoint Templates). Once an image has been imported into a project, you can resize it, crop it, and apply multiple effects to it. You'll also find that the image is represented in Captivate's Library. Once there, a Library object can quickly be dragged to any slide.

Student Activity: Insert, Resize, and Restore an Image

1. Open **Introduction** from the **Captivate9Data** folder.

   The Introduction project is a sample project provided by **Next Turn Consulting**, a training company specializing in improving communication, leadership, and results. It is the first of six modules in the CALM in Conflict© eLearning project. More information about Next Turn can be found at www.nextturnconsulting.com.

2. Preview the project.

   The project is loaded with images, audio, captions, and object effects. During the immediate lessons, you will learn how to add and format some of the images you see in this project. You learned how to work with Text Captions beginning on page 66. You will learn about audio soon (page 139). And you will learn about object effects on page 170.

3. Close the preview.

4. Close the project (do not save if prompted).

5. Open **ImageMe** from the **Captivate9Data** folder.

   This project is nearly identical to the Introduction project. Of course, some of the images are missing... and that's where you come in. Let's add some images to this project.

6. Insert an image onto slide 1.

   ❑ if necessary, go to slide **1**

   ❑ choose **Media > Image**

   ❑ navigate to the **Captivate9Data** folder

   ❑ from the **images_animation** folder, open **Skybackground.png**

   The image, which is quite large, is inserted in the middle of the slide. The other slide objects are behind the newly inserted image. The image is so big, its left edge is hanging off the left side of the slide and is bleeding onto the Pasteboard. (As first mentioned on page 16, the Pasteboard is the large area surrounding your slide. It can be used for items that you aren't ready to delete. Objects on the Pasteboard do not appear in the published version of your lesson. However, if part of an object is on the slide and part of the object is on the Pasteboard, you will end up with a nice bleed effect you've likely seen in print publications such as magazines and newspapers.)

7. Change the slide's view magnification.

❏ choose **View > Magnification > 50%**

8. Manually resize an image.

❏ with the image you just inserted on slide 1 selected, position your mouse pointer over the resizing handle in the **upper right** of the image

❏ drag the handle down and to the left to make the image much **smaller**

Although resizing an image by dragging its handles is perfectly fine in some instances, you could easily end up with a resized image that is out of proportion. You'll learn a better way to resize in just a minute. First, let's get the image back to its original size.

9. Reset an image size.

❏ with the image is still selected, select the **Style** tab on the **Properties Inspector**

❏ click the **Reset To Original Size** button

The image should be the back to its original size. The location of the image has changed, which you will alter next. I often receive questions as to the value of the Reset To Original Size button. Many people believe that it would be just as easy to Undo the image resize as an alternative to clicking the Reset To Original Size button. It's true that clicking the Reset button and using the Undo command achieves the same result. However, the Undo command is valuable only as long as the project is open. If you close the project and save your changes, the Undo command won't work when you reopen the project. The Reset button always works.

Student Activity: Transform an Image

1. Ensure that the **ImageMe** project is still open.

2. Use the Properties Inspector to change the size of an image.

   ☐ with the **Skybackground** image on slide **1** still selected, click the **Options** tab on the Properties Inspector

   ☐ in the **Transform** area, ensure that **Constrain proportions** is selected

   You are about to make the image a bit larger by changing the W value. With Constrain proportions selected, the height of the image changes proportionally when you change the width.

   ☐ change the **W** value to **1400**

   The H value should automatically change to **649**.

3. Specify a specific slide position for the image.

   ☐ on the **Transform** area, change the **X** value to **-412**

   ☐ change the **Y** value to **-3**

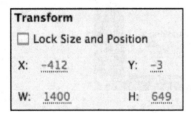

   The X value controls the horizontal position of the selected object; the Y value controls the vertical slide position. The image should now be bleeding onto the Pasteboard (mostly on the left side of the slide). Because the image is so large, you cannot see the slide objects that were on the slide before you imported the image. You'll send the image behind the other slide objects next.

4. Send the main image behind the other slide objects.

   ☐ with the cloud image still selected, choose **Modify > Arrange > Send to Back**

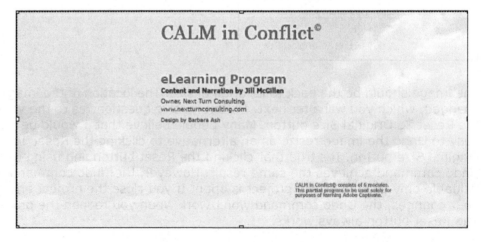

Images Confidence Check

1. Right-click the cloud image and choose **Show for the rest of the slide** (so that the image is on the slide along with all of the other slide objects).

   Note: When right-clicking the image, be careful. There are several objects on the slide. By right-clicking the edge of the image, you'll be sure you're editing the timing for the image, not one of the other slide objects.

2. On the **Timing Inspector**, **Transition** area, change the **Transition** to **Fade In Only**.

3. Still working on slide **1**, insert the image named **Jill.bmp**.

4. Transform the image as follows:

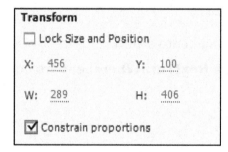

Your slide should look like this:

5. Set the image to **Show for the rest of the slide**.

6. Change the **Transition** to **Fade In Only**.

7. Insert the **NextTurnLogo** image onto slide **1**.

8. Transform the **NextTurnLogo** as follows:

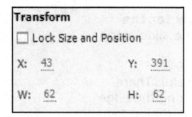

9. Set the Timing and Transition for the **NextTurnLogo** as follows:

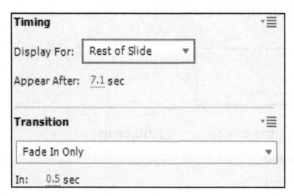

10. Insert the **NextTurnWhereLeaders** image onto slide **1**.

11. Transform the **X** and **Y** attributes for the **NextTurnWhereLeaders** image as follows:

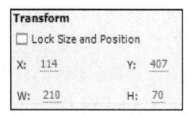

12. Set the Timing and Transition for the **NextTurnWhereLeaders** image as follows:

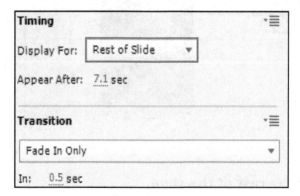

13. Insert the **BannerBottomSlide1** image onto slide **1**.

14. Transform the **BannerBottomSlide1** image as follows:

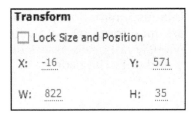

15. Set the Timing and Transition for the **BannerBottomSlide1** image as follows:

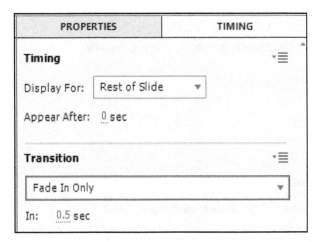

The first slide should look like the picture below. Remember that much of the background image is bleeding off the left side of the slide, which is the reason things look a bit unbalanced. For a more accurate view of what your learners will see, observe the Filmstrip thumbnail of slide 1 (where you'll see that the left edge is cut off) or preview the first few slides.

16. Save and close the project.

The Library

Your slides can contain audio, background images, images, animations, linked PowerPoint presentations, and more. Those assets are monitored by Captivate's Library. Once the Library is opened, you can add previously imported assets onto any slide by dragging the object's name from the Library and onto the slide.

Student Activity: Use the Library

1. Open the **MoreImageMe** project.

2. Show the Library.

   ☐ from the top right of the Captivate window, click **Library**

3. Use the Library to add an image to slide 2.

   ☐ on the Library, scroll down to the **Images** folder

   All of the images you added during the previous activities in this module are listed in the Library. There are also images you didn't add—these were added by the original developer who worked on this project.

   Notice that there is a **Use Count** column in the Library.

   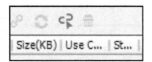

   Every time you use an image in the project, the Use Count goes up by one. If you delete every occurrence of the image from the project slides, a copy of the image still remains in the Library. Because the developer of this project inserted and then deleted slide images, some of the images in the Library show a **0** as a Use Count.

   ☐ from the middle of the Images folder on the Library, select **BrandingLogo.png** (if necessary, make the **Name** column wider so you can see the names of the images)

   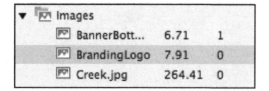

   At the top of the Library, notice that there is a preview of the selected image.

❑ go to slide **2**

❑ drag **BrandingLogo** from the Library and onto slide 2

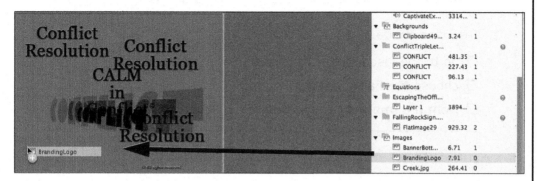

Now that the image is on slide 2, notice in the Library that the **Use Count** column for the Library asset updates to show 1.

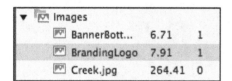

4. View specific image usage.

❑ in the Library, select **BrandingLogo**

❑ at the top of the Library, click the **Usage** command

The Usage dialog box opens, letting you know where the image is being used.

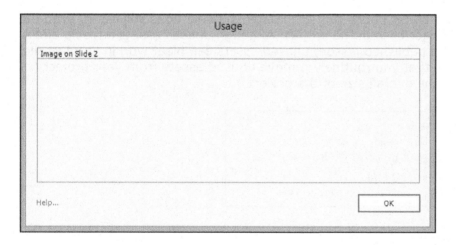

❑ click the **OK** button

Student Activity: Manage Unused Project Assets

1. Ensure that the **MoreImageMe** project is still open.

2. Insert an image.

   ❏ go to the last slide in the project

   ❏ choose **Media > Image**

   ❏ from the **images_animation** folder, open **betty_baby.jpg**

3. Delete the betty_baby image you just inserted on the slide.

   In the Library, notice that the image you deleted is still listed, even though it is no longer used in the project. Although unused assets have no effect on the size of a published lesson, unused assets can bloat working project files. I suggest that you routinely remove unused assets from your project (which lowers the overall size of the project).

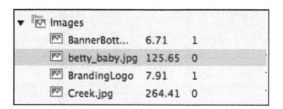

4. Delete unused Library items.

   ❏ from the top of the Library, click the **Select Unused Items** tool

   Three Library objects are unused. They are now selected and can be deleted.

   ❏ from the top of the Library, click the **Delete** tool 🗑

   ❏ click **Yes** to confirm the deletion

Image Editing

Although Captivate is not an image editing program like Adobe Photoshop, you can control several aspects of an image, including flipping it horizontally and vertically, controlling its rotation, setting its brightness and contrast, and cropping it. During the next activity, you will crop part of the image you inserted onto the second slide.

Student Activity: Crop and Rename an Image

1. Ensure that the **MoreImageMe** project is still open.

2. Crop an image.

   ❑ go to slide **2**

   ❑ select the image you added to the slide earlier

   Clearly, this image needs your help... nobody is asking how the "Ooops" text got into the image, but it's got to go.

   ❑ on the **Properties Inspector**, click the **Style** tab

   ❑ click the **Edit Image** button

   The Resize/Crop Image dialog box opens.

   ❑ on the right side of the dialog box, select **Crop**

   ❑ if necessary, deselect **Constraint Proportion**

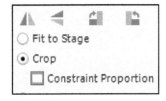

   ❑ on the image, drag the bottom, right resizing handle **up and to the left** just enough to remove the words "Ooops. Crop Me" and the white space surrounding them

   ❑ click the **OK** button

The words "Ooops. Crop Me" have been cropped out of the image. Because you deselected Constraint Proportion, you were able to control exactly how much of the image you cropped.

On the Library, notice that there is a second BrandingLogo image (the original and the one you cropped). The newer image, BrandingLogo(2), needs a new name.

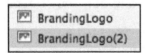

3. Rename an image.

   ❏ on the Library, right-click **BrandingLogo.png(2)** and choose **Rename**

   ❏ change the name to **BrandingLogoCropped**

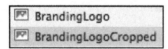

Student Activity: Remove a Background Color

1. Ensure that the **MoreImageMe** project is still open.

2. On slide **2**, notice that the cropped NextTurn image (BrandingLogoCropped) has a white background. You'll remove the white so that the image works with the background.

3. Remove a background color from an image.

   ☐ with the NextTurn image selected, on the **Properties Inspector**, **Style** tab, click the rectangle to the right of the **Make the selected color transparent** icon

   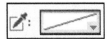

   ☐ select the **Eyedropper** tool

   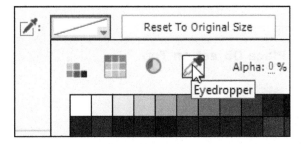

   ☐ using the Eyedropper tool, click in the white part of the NextTurn image

   The white part of the image should be deleted.

   Admittedly, the results aren't perfect. For instance, there's still a bit of white around the letters. Intense image editing would be best performed in a dedicated image editing program like Adobe Photoshop. But that's not the point here... I love the fact that if you're in a pinch, there's a great deal you can do directly within Captivate that adequately gets the job done.

Properties Confidence Check

1. Transform the BrandingLogoCropped image as follows:

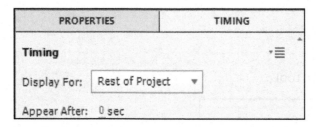

Transform		
☐ Lock Size and Position		
X: 659	Y: 567	
W: 100	H: 21	

2. Set the **Timing** for the NextTurn image to **Display For** to **Rest of Project**

PROPERTIES	TIMING
Timing	▾☰
Display For: Rest of Project ▾	
Appear After: 0 sec	

3. From the Timing area, select **Place Object on Top**.

☑ Place Object on Top

4. Change the Transition to **No Transition**.

Transition	▾☰
No Transition ▾	

5. Starting with slide **2**, preview the next five slides.

   As the slides play, notice that the logo appears in the same location on every slide. Using the **Rest of Project** Display time is a handy trick that lets you repeat slide objects without having to create master slides (a topic that I cover in *Adobe Captivate 9: Beyond the Essentials*) or pasting the images on every slide. The **Place Object on Top** option ensures that the BrandingLogoCropped image always appears in front of competing slide objects.

6. Close the preview.

7. Still working on slide 2, set the timing for the "All rights reserved" text caption to **Display For** to **Rest of Project**

8. Preview the next five slides.

   Now both the caption and the image appear on every slide.

9. Close the preview and save your work.

Characters

Finding quality royalty-free photographs, especially of cut out people that you can use throughout your lessons as learner guides, is always a challenge. Fortunately, Captivate comes with a wonderful assortment of Characters (via the Media tool). There are multiple Character categories (such as Business and Medicine). Each category contains multiple models and poses.

Student Activity: Insert Characters

1. Ensure that the **MoreImageMe** project is still open.

2. Go to slide **5**.

3. Insert a Character.

   ❏ choose **Media > Characters**

   The Characters dialog box opens.

   ❏ from the **Category** drop-down menu, choose **Business**

   ❏ from the left side of the dialog box, select **any character**

   ❏ from the middle of the dialog box, select **any pose**

   ❏ from the right side of the dialog box, select **Half**

   ❏ click the **OK** button

   Note: If you receive an alert message about missing assets after clicking the OK button, you can download the missing Characters for free. However, the assets are large and could take a significant amount of time to download. Because the first pose for every Character is usually available, consider using that pose and download the assets later.

Characters Confidence Check

1. Still working in the **MoreImageMe** project, resize and position the Character until your slide is similar to the image below.

2. Insert a second character onto the slide and position and resize it similar to the image below.

Assets

Adobe teamed with the eLearning Brothers and Captivate includes thousands of free eLearning Brother assets (templates, cut out people, etc.) that you can use in your projects. Download images from the eLearning Brothers website are automatically installed in the Media category when you access Characters.

Student Activity: Insert Assets

1. Ensure that the **MoreImageMe** project is still open.

2. Download an asset from the eLearning Brothers website.

   ☐ on the toolbar, click **Assets**

   The Assets screen appears. If you already have an eLearning Brothers account, you can use your existing credentials and log in. If you do not have an account, use the **Create Account** button at the right and create one now.

Once you've logged in, you will have free access to more than 30,000 assets, including cutout people (similar to the Characters you inserted a moment ago), games, and interactions. These assets are free with your Captivate 9 license.

   ☐ from the menu, click **Cutout People**

❏ select any character you like

❏ select any pose you like

❏ from the **right side** of the dialog box, click the **Download** button next to the image size you like (in the image below, I've selected the largest image)

❏ once the download is complete, click the **OK** button

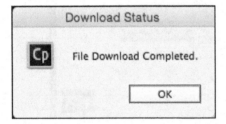

❏ click the **Close** button to close the Assets window

The asset has been downloaded and automatically loaded into Captivate's Media library. The asset is not, however, automatically inserted onto a slide. You'll manually insert the asset onto a slide next.

3. Insert the downloaded asset onto a slide.

   ☐ if necessary, go to slide **5**

   ☐ choose **Media > Characters**

   ☐ from the **Category** drop-down menu, choose **Assets**

   ☐ select the asset you downloaded (in the image below you can see the asset I just downloaded, along with other assets I've downloaded over the past few days)

   ☐ from the right side of the dialog box, select **Half**

   ☐ click the **OK** button

   At this point, you could move and resize the Character just as you did the other assets you've added previously.

4. Save and close the project.

Smart Shapes

If you're a PowerPoint user, you've long appreciated the ability to draw just about any kind of shape you need on your slides using AutoShapes. In Captivate, you have a similar ability via the Smart Shapes feature. You'll find myriad shapes from which to choose, including Callouts, Banners, and other wacky shapes.

Student Activity: Insert a Cloud Callout

1. Open the **SmartShapeMe** project from the **Captivate9Data** folder.

2. Insert a Cloud Callout Smart Shape.

    ❏ go to slide **5**

    ❏ choose **Shapes > Cloud Callout**

    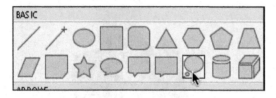

    ❏ using the Cloud Callout Smart Shape, draw a large callout from the image of the woman diagonally **up** and to the **right**

Smart Shapes Confidence Check

1. Insert a Cloud Callout Smart Shape above the image of the man.

2. After drawing the second callout above the man, you're probably concerned with the direction of the callout... it's not pointing at the man. That's easily fixed. Drag the bottom **yellow resizing handle** toward the man's head to change the direction of the Smart Shape.

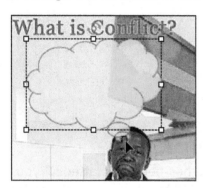

3. Double-click within the first Cloud Callout (the callout above the woman) and type the following:

RESOLUTION:

The act of resolving or determining a course of action

4. Double-click within the second Cloud Callout and type the following:

CONFLICT:

To come into collision or disagreement

5. Select either one of the Cloud Callouts and, on the **Style** tab of the Properties Inspector, change the font to **Verdana**.

6. Change the font size to **17**.

7. Change the text alignment to **Align Center**.

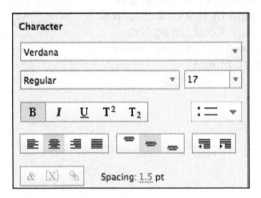

8. Change the **Spacing** to **1.5**

    Notice that only the selected Smart Shape has been formatted. If you want the other Smart Shape to use the same formatting, you'll need to update the [Default Smart Shape Style].

9. Click the menu to the right of **Style Name** and choose **Save changes to Existing Style**.

10. Save and close the project.

Background Editing

If there are problems with your slide backgrounds (perhaps a rogue author has doodled on the slide), you could re-record just the slide containing the problem. Although this would fix the problem, it might take a significant amount of work to get your screen in just the right position so you can re-create the screen capture. Even if you think you've got everything just perfect, there might be subtle differences between the original screen capture and the new one—differences you might not notice until it's too late.

If your background contains something you want to delete and your background is any solid color, you can create a mask (insert an image or highlight box using the same color as the background, cover the problem, and then merge the image or highlight box into the background).

Student Activity: Create an Image Mask

1. Open **MaskPhotoshopMe** from the **Captivate9Data** folder.

2. Go to slide **8**.

    There is an image on the slide that needs your attention... it's an image that isn't just sitting on the slide; it's been merged with the slide background. Getting rid of the image isn't going to be as simple as selecting and deleting it. Because the image is part of the slide background, you'll need to create a mask to hide it.

    ☐ choose **Objects > Highlight Box**

    A highlight box appears in the middle of the slide.

    ☐ reposition and resize the Highlight Box until it completely covers the doodle

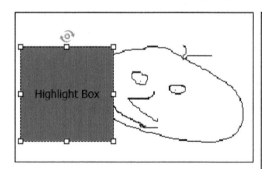 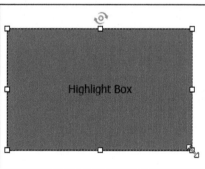

    In a moment, you will be merging the Highlight Box onto the slide's background, making the doodle art just a bad memory. But not so fast. If you merge the Highlight Box now, the doodle will be gone, only to be replaced by a blue box. Let's change the color of the Highlight Box from blue to white and then proceed with the merge process.

3. Change the color of the Highlight Box to white.

   ❏ with the Highlight Box still selected, locate the **Fill** area on the Properties Inspector (it's on the **Style** tab)

   ❏ click the **Fill** tool and change the color to **white**

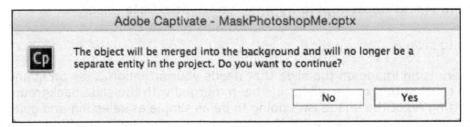

4. Merge the image into the background.

   ❏ with the white highlight box still selected, choose **Modify > Merge with the background**

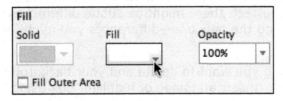

   ❏ click the **Yes** button

   The Highlight Box is gone. The doodle art is gone. And all is right with the world.

5. Save your work.

Integrating Photoshop

You can import native Adobe Photoshop files (PSD files) directly onto Captivate slides, even if you don't own or use Photoshop. When you import a PSD file, the layers created in Photoshop are preserved, giving you incredible control over how and when the objects on the layers appear on a slide.

Student Activity: Delete a Slide Background

1. Ensure that the **MaskPhotoshopMe** project is still open.

2. Delete the background image for slide 1.

   ❏ using the Filmstrip, select slide **1**

   ❏ choose **Edit > Find Background in the Library**

   The Library opens and the **ReplaceMe** background image is selected.

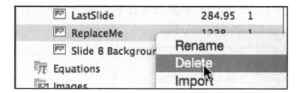

   ❏ right-click the **ReplaceMe** image in the Library selected and choose **Delete**

   Because the image is being used by slide **1**, you'll be asked to confirm the action.

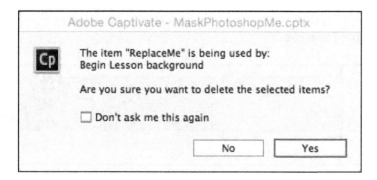

   ❏ click the **Yes** button

   The slide's background has been deleted. Even so, notice that the slide and the slide objects (the button and background audio) are intact.

Student Activity: Work with Photoshop Layers

1. Ensure that the **MaskPhotoshopMe** project is still open.

2. Import a Photoshop file onto slide 1.

   ❑ with slide **1** selected, choose **File > Import > Photoshop File**

   ❑ from the **Captivate9Data** folder, open the **images_animation** folder

   ❑ open **LessonBackground.psd**

   The Import dialog box appears. This Photoshop file contains layers named Logo, SkillsDrills, etc. You could elect to flatten the layers (by selecting Import as Flattened Image), which is exactly what the slide contained before you deleted its background image a moment ago. The advantage of importing the layers is that you can control when each object on each layer appears on your slide, paving the way for some interesting transition effects in your Captivate project.

   ❑ from the **Import as** area at the right side of the dialog box, ensure that **Layers** is selected

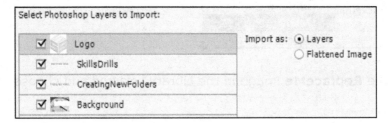

   ❑ click the **OK** button

   Display the Timeline and notice that each of the Photoshop layers has been assigned a row in the Timeline.

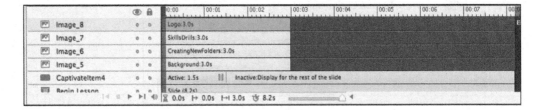

3. Extend the playtime for the Photoshop layers.

   ❑ still working on slide **1**, select **Logo** on the Timeline

   ❑ press and hold [**Shift**] on your keyboard

   ❑ click once on the last image on the Timeline (**Background**)

   ❑ release the [**Shift**] key

   All of the images (Logo through Background) should be selected.

   ❑ choose **Modify > Show for the rest of the slide**

All timing for all of the selected objects has been adjusted so that they play for the same amount of time as the slide duration.

4. Control when slide objects appear on the slide.

   ❏ still working on slide **1**, go to the Timeline and select the **Logo** object

   ❏ on the **Timing Inspector**, change the **Appear After** to **1** sec

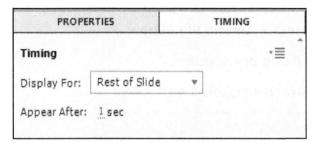

Layers Confidence Check

1. Adjust the timing for the **SkillsDrills** object so that it Appears after 2 seconds.

2. Adjust the timing for the **CreatingNewFolders** object so that it Appears after 3 seconds.

3. On the Timeline, select the button and choose **Modify > Arrange > Bring to Front**.

4. Adjust the timing for the **button** object so that it Appears after 4 seconds.

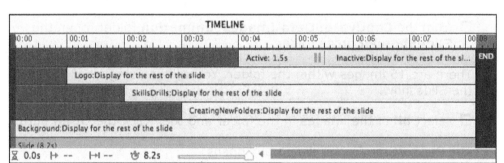

5. Starting with slide **1**, preview the Next 5 slides to test the timing of the layers.

6. Close the preview, save, and close the project.

Image Slideshows

If you have a collection of images on your hard drive or server, you can use Captivate's Image slideshow feature to quickly create a nifty slideshow.

Student Activity: Create an Image Slideshow

1. Create an Image slideshow project.

   ❏ choose **File > New Project > Image Slideshow**

   The New Image Slideshow dialog box appears.

   ❏ from the **Select** drop-down menu, select **640 x 480**

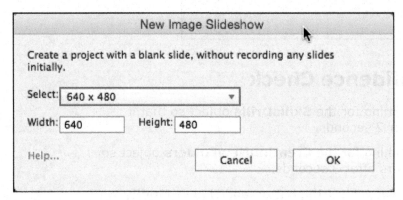

   ❏ click the **OK** button

2. Find the images to be used in the slideshow.

   ❏ from the **Captivate9Data\images_animation** folder, open the **SlideShowPictures** folder

   There are 15 images within the folder. You will be using all of the images in the Slideshow.

   ❏ select **all** of the images in the folder and then click the **Open** button

   The Resize/Crop Image dialog box opens.

   ❏ click the **OK** button

   The images are imported into a new untitled project and set as the background on each slide.

Transitions Confidence Check

1. Preview the project.

   The slideshow works, but the slides move along just a bit too quickly.

2. Close the preview.

3. On the Filmstrip, select the first slide.

4. Scroll down the Filmstrip until you see the last slide.

5. Press [**shift**] and select the last slide. (All of the slides should now be selected, and you can release the [**shift**] key.)

6. On the Timing Inspector, change the **Slide Duration** for the slides to **5** seconds.

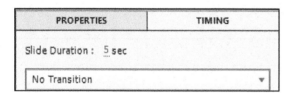

7. Preview the project.

   The timing is better. But wouldn't it be even better to have a transition between one slide and the next? You bet...

8. Select the first slide on the Filmstrip.

9. From the **Transition** drop-down menu on the **Timing Inspector**, select any **Transition** you like.

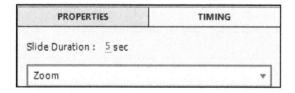

10. Repeat this process for a few more of the slides.

11. When finished, preview the project.

12. Once satisfied with the transitions, close the project. (You can save the project to the **Captivate9Data** folder with any name that you like, or you can close the project without saving it.)

Notes

iCONLOGiC

"Skills and Drills" Learning

Module 6: Pointers, Paths, Boxes, and Buttons

In This Module You Will Learn About:

And You Will Learn To:

Mouse Effects

If your lesson is intended to demonstrate an application, including the Mouse pointer is a good idea. If you do include the Mouse pointer, you can also include a visual Mouse click and click sound that further enhances the user experience.

Student Activity: Control Mouse Effects

1. Open **MouseVisualMe** from the **Captivate9Data** folder.

2. Preview the project.

   ☐ choose **Preview > Project**

   This project is a demonstration showing new computer users how to create a new folder on the computer. The slides contain images (you learned how to add images beginning on page 84) and Text Captions (you learned how to add captions on page 66). As the Mouse moves from slide to slide, there is no visual indicator that a click is occurring, and no sound effect to accompany the click.

3. Add a click sound to the Mouse on slide 4.

   ☐ close the preview and then go to slide **4**

   This is where the Mouse goes to the **File** menu and the menu is clicked. It's the perfect place to add both a visual Mouse click and click sound.

   ☐ on the **Timeline** double-click the **Mouse** object

   ☐ on the **Properties Inspector**, select **Mouse Click Sound**

   ☐ ensure **Single-click** is selected from the drop-down menu

   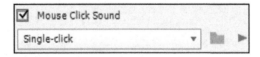

4. Add a visual Mouse click to the Mouse pointer on slide 4.

   ☐ ensure the **Mouse** on slide **4** is still selected

   ☐ on the **Properties Inspector**, select **Show Mouse Click**

   ☐ select **Custom** from the drop-down menu and select any of the Mouse clicks you like from the drop-down menu (you can preview the Mouse click visual by clicking the Play button to the right of the selection)

   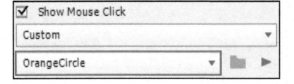

Visual Click Confidence Check

1. Go to slide **3** and preview the next five slides. (**Preview > Next 5 slides**)

   When slide **4** plays, you should see and hear the Mouse click.

2. Add a visual Mouse click and Mouse click sound to the Mouse pointer on slides **5**, **6**, and **8**.

3. Use the Timing Inspector to change the Transition for slide **2** to **Wipe**.

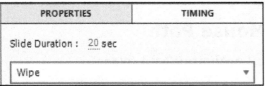

4. Save your work.

5. Preview the project.

   As the lesson plays, pay particular attention to the **Wipe** transition you added that softens the abrupt jump between slides 1 and 2. In addition, notice the visual Mouse clicks and sounds you added.

6. When the preview is finished, close the preview.

7. Save and close the project.

Pointer Paths and Types

When you record a lesson using Captivate, every move you make with the Mouse can be recorded, including menu selections, dialog box selections, and the path your Mouse takes as you move it around the screen. Captivate includes the ability to easily change the pointer path without having to re-record the lesson.

After you record a Demonstration (you learned how on page 48) that includes the Mouse cursor, you can change the way the Mouse pointer looks on a single Captivate slide or throughout the project. The pointer can be changed to a variety of icons, such as a hand, a vertical resize pointer, or a drag pointer. If you are not happy with the pointer icons that come with Captivate, you can select any system pointer or existing CUR (cursor) file on your hard drive or network as the pointer image.

Student Activity: Edit a Mouse Path

1. Open **PointerPathMe** from the **Captivate9Data** folder.

2. Hide slide objects.

   ☐ go to slide **3**

   ☐ on the **Timeline**, look to the left of the caption containing the words "Watch as..."

   ☐ click **Show/Hide Item** (the little circle just beneath the eyeball icon)

   The little circle turns into a red X when clicked. The Show/Hide Item is a toggle. To Show an item, click the red X, and it returns to the shape of a circle.

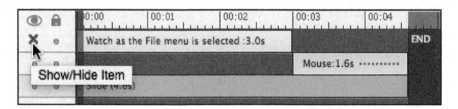

With the selected caption hidden, it's easier to focus on the slide's Mouse pointer. Notice that the tip of the pointer (the tip of the Mouse pointer is often referred to as the "hot spot") is pointing just to the right of the "e" in "File." It might look a bit better if the hot spot of the Mouse pointer is optically centered over the word "File."

3. Edit the pointer path.

   ❏ drag the Mouse pointer **up** and to the **left** just a bit so that it is more optically centered over the word **File**

During the recording process (you learned about recording screen actions on page 46), it's possible that you made a mistake and clicked the wrong part of the screen. In that instance, Captivate creates a screen capture, and your Mouse is shown in the wrong part of the screen. *Ouch!* You've just learned that you can move the Mouse pointer location in Captivate *after the recording process*. How slick is that? Re-record a lesson? I don't think so!

4. Go to slide 4.

   Notice that the Mouse pointer on slide 4 didn't get the memo from the Mouse pointer on slide 3 (informing it that it needs to move up and to the left). You can get a better look at the problem by switching between slides 3 and 4, and you see the pointer jump between the two slides. Hold on for a bit of magic as you tell the pointer on slide 4 to match the position of the pointer on slide 3.

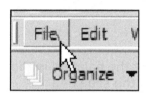

5. Align the slide position of the Mouse pointer with the previous slide.

   ❏ still working on slide **4**, select the Mouse

   ❏ choose **Modify > Mouse > Align to Previous slide**

   The position of the Mouse pointer on slide 4 should now match the position you established for the Mouse pointer on slide 3. Without this wonderful feature, you would have been forced to drag the pointer on slide 4 a bit at a time, and then constantly switch between slides 3 and 4 to ensure that the alignment is perfect. The **Align to** feature makes quick work of the process.

6. Return to slide **3** and show the text caption that you hid a moment ago.

7. Change the Mouse pointer type.

   ❏ go to slide **9**

   Notice the Mouse pointer type is a standard white pointer.

   ❏ select the Mouse

☐ on the **Properties Inspector**, **Display** area, click the **>** twice and then select the **Hand Pointer**

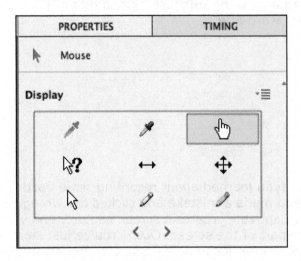

On the slide, the Mouse pointer now looks like a hand pointer. This change affects only the pointer on slide **9**.

Note: If you wanted to use this pointer type on all of the pointers in the current project, you could right-click the pointer on the slide and choose **Use the current mouse pointer for all slides**.

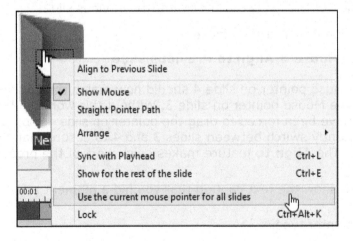

8. Save your work.

Highlight Boxes

In addition to serving as background masks (you learned how to create a mask on page 105), Highlight Boxes provide a great way to grab the learner's attention... they are especially helpful if a slide is cluttered. Like most objects in Captivate, you can control the appearance of Highlight Boxes via Object Styles the length of time they are on stage via the Timeline or the Timing Inspector.

Student Activity: Clone an Object Style

1. Ensure that the **PointerPathMe** project is still open.

2. Clone an existing style.

   ❏ choose **Edit > Object Style Manager**

   ❏ at the far left of the dialog box, click the triangle to expand the **Standard Objects** area

   ❏ select **Highlight Box**

   ❏ from the middle column, select **[Default Blue Highlight Box Style]**

   ❏ at the bottom of the column, click the **Clone** button

   The selected style has been duplicated. You can now give the duplicate any name you like and then edit its attributes.

   ❏ in the Name area at the right, change the name to **Custom Highlight Box Style**

   ❏ from the **Fill & Stroke** area, select any Fill, Stroke Color, and Width you like

   ❏ change the Transition to **Fade In Only**

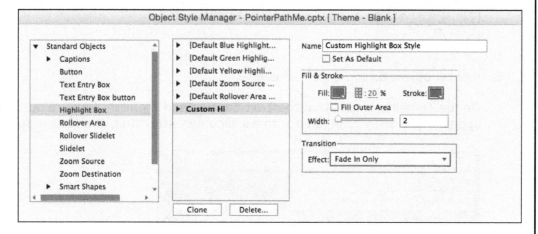

   ❏ click the **OK** button

Student Activity: Insert a Highlight Box

1. Ensure that the **PointerPathMe** project is still open.

2. Insert a Highlight Box.

   ❏ go to slide **3**

   ❏ choose **Objects > Highlight Box**

   The New Highlight Box box appears on the slide using the attributes of the [Default Blue Highlight Box Style].

3. Apply a different style to the new Highlight Box.

   ❏ from the **Style Name** drop-down menu on the **Properties Inspector**, choose **Custom Highlight Box Style**

   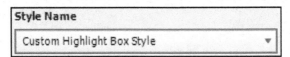

   The appearance of the selected Highlight Box should match the attributes of the style you created a moment ago. If you are unhappy with the appearance of the object, you can at any time return to the Object Style Manager, select the style, and edit it.

4. Resize and reposition the Highlight Box.

   ❏ on the slide, drag the Highlight Box **up** and to the **left** and resize it so that it covers just the **File** menu

5. Review object timing on the Timeline.

   On the Timeline, notice that the Text Caption and Highlight Box are both set to appear right away and play for three seconds. After that, the Mouse appears.

   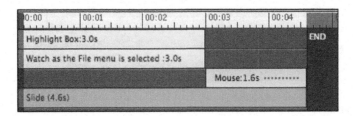

6. Preview a single slide.

   ❏ choose **Preview > Play slide**

   As expected, the Highlight Box fades in as the slide plays and stays around as long as the text caption. Then the Mouse does its thing. However, the timing for the caption is a bit off. You might have noticed that the caption stuck around a tiny bit longer than the Highlight Box. The reason? The Highlight Box has a Transition of Fade In Only. The caption's Transition is set to Fade In and Out. You'll change that next.

7. Update and then save changes to an existing style.

    ❑ select the **Text Caption** on slide **3**

    ❑ on the **Timing Inspector,** change the **Transition** to **Fade In Only**

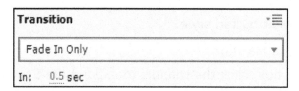

    ❑ select the **Properties Inspector**

    From the Style Name area at the top of the Properties Inspector, notice the plus sign to the left of the Default Caption Style. The plus sign indicates changes have been made to the selected caption that do not match the attributes of the style.

    ❑ click the menu at the right of **Style Name** and choose **Save changes to Existing Style** button

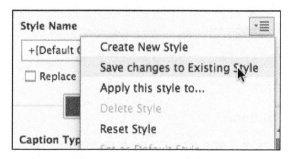

    The attributes for all of the captions in the project have been updated and now reflect the Fade In Only Transition.

8. Play the slide.

    Now the timing and effects for both the Highlight Box and Text Caption match.

9. Save the project.

Image Buttons

Earlier in this book (page 32) you were introduced to buttons. During the next few activities, you'll take a deeper look at buttons, including controlling timing and adding Image buttons.

Student Activity: Insert an Image Button

1. Ensure that the **PointerPathMe** project is still open.

2. Set Image buttons as the default button style.

   ☐ choose **Edit > Object Style Manager**

   ☐ at the far left of the dialog box, click the triangle to expand the **Standard Objects** area

   ☐ select **Button**

   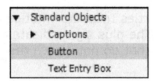

   ☐ from the middle of the dialog box, select **[Default Image Button Style]**

   ☐ from the right side of the dialog box, select **Set As Default**

   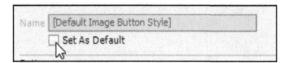

3. Select an image for the image button.

   ☐ from the **Button** area, scroll down and select any image you like (when making your selection, consider that the button will be used by the learner to get to the next slide... the image you choose should reflect the button's intended Action)

   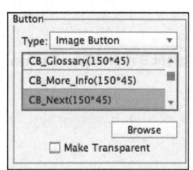

   ☐ click the **OK** button

4. Insert the image button onto a slide.

   ❏ select slide **1**

   ❏ choose **Interactions > Button**

   An image button is added to the middle of the slide. Next you'll control what happens when the learner interacts with the button. The **Actions** tab on the **Properties Inspector** has several options in the **On Success** drop-down menu. For instance, you can select **Continue**. With this Action selected, the slide continues to play the remaining time on the Timeline before the learner is taken to the next slide. Alternatively, you can elect to jump the learner to a specific slide in the project. Or you can elect to have the button play a sound. In this instance, you'd like the button to take the learner to the next slide when the button is clicked.

5. Set the button's Action.

   ❏ ensure the Button is selected

   ❏ on the **Properties Inspector**, select the **Actions** tab

   ❏ from the **On Success** drop-down menu, ensure **Go to the next slide** is selected

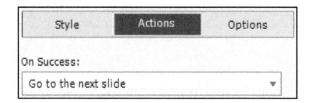

   Next you'll set the timing for the button. Although you can do whatever you want with the timing, in this instance, you'd like the button to appear on the slide right away and stick around as long as the slide plays.

6. Set the button's Timing.

   ❏ ensure the button is still selected

   ❏ select the **Timing Inspector**

   ❏ from the **Display For** drop-down menu, select **Rest of Slide**

   ❏ ensure that **Appear After** is set to **0 sec**

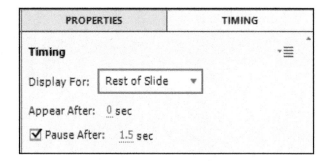

7. Resize and reposition the button similar to the picture below.

8. Preview the Next 5 slides.

    As the first slide plays, notice that the action stops too soon—not all of the slide objects have had a chance to appear. You will fix that problem next.

9. Close the preview.

Student Activity: Control Appear After Timing

1. Ensure that the **PointerPathMe** project is still open.

2. Edit a button's Properties so that it pauses the slide after an appropriate amount of time.

    ☐ select the Button on slide **1**

    ☐ select the **Timing Inspector**

    ☐ change **Pause After** to **4.5** seconds

    Setting **Pause After** to 4.5 seconds gives the other slide objects enough time to appear on the slide before the slide action stops.

    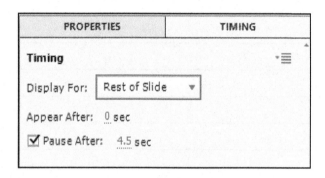

3. Edit the Properties of the button to show a Hand Cursor.

    ☐ select the **Properties Inspector**

    ☐ on the **Actions** tab, **Others** area, select **Hand Cursor**

    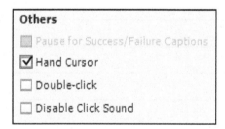

4. Preview the First 5 slides.

    After slide 1 appears, notice that all of the slide elements show up on the slide, and then the lesson stops—waiting for you to click the button.

5. Position your Mouse pointer over the button and notice that your Mouse pointer changes to a hand Mouse cursor—thanks to the **Hand Cursor** option you selected.

6. Click the button to jump to the next slide in the lesson.

7. Close the preview, and then save and close the project.

Notes

iCONLOGiC

"Skills and Drills" Learning

Module 7: Rollovers and Zooms

In This Module You Will Learn About:

And You Will Learn To:

Rollover Captions

You learned how to create Text Captions beginning on page 66. Although similar to Text Captions, Rollover Captions consist of two things: a caption and a rectangular "hot spot." The Rollover Captions appear in your published projects only when the learner moves the mouse over the hot spot. Rollover Captions are especially useful for creating tooltips within an application. To see an example of a working tooltip, point to any tool on any Captivate toolbar (the text that appears is a tooltip).

Student Activity: Insert a Rollover Caption

1. Open **MouseSkills** from the **Captivate9Data** folder.

2. Preview the project.

   This project has similar elements, such as graphics, buttons, and object timing that you have learned to create during previous lessons. During the lessons that follow, you will be inserting Rollover Captions on slide **2** (and Rollover Images on slide **3**).

3. Close the preview.

4. Observe the styles used for the Rollover Captions in the Object Style Manager.

   ❏ choose **Edit > Object Style Manager**

   ❏ from the **top left** of the dialog box, expand **Standard Objects**

   ❏ expand **Captions**

   ❏ from the Captions area, select **Rollover Caption**

   ❏ in the **middle** of the dialog box, notice that there is a caption called **RolloverCaptions**

   ❏ at the **top right** of the dialog box, notice that **RolloverCaptions** is **Set As Default**

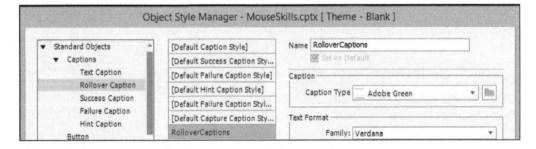

The **RolloverCaptions** style is an Object Style that I created by cloning the Default Caption Style. You learned about cloning on page 119.

   ❏ lower down the **Standard Objects** list, select **Rollover Area**

   ❏ at the right of the dialog box, observe the settings in the **Fill & Stroke** area and **Transition** areas

I've already set up the style for you and it will result in a transparent rollover area. If you'd like a refresher on working with the Object Style Manager and styles in general, review the activities beginning on page 72.

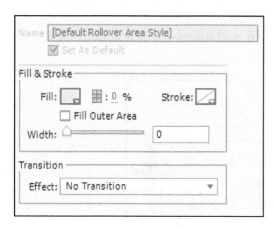

❑ click the **Cancel** button

5. Insert a Rollover Caption onto a slide.

❑ go to slide **2**

You're going to be adding rollover areas and captions for each of the images on this slide.

❑ choose **Objects > Rollover Caption**

Two things appear on your slide: a Rollover Caption and a Rollover Area. Both objects are formatted to match the styles you just reviewed in the Object Style Manager.

❑ type **Excellent, you hit number 1!** into the Text Caption

6. Change the caption's Callout.

❑ with just the **Rollover Caption** selected, go to the **Properties Inspector**, **Style** tab

❑ select the first **Callout**

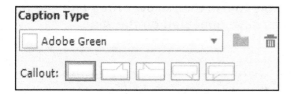

7. Move and resize the Rollover Caption.

❑ drag the **Rollover Caption** just **above** and to the **right** of the image of the number **1**

❑ resize the **Rollover Caption** to suit your taste

8. Move and resize the Rollover Area.

   ❑ drag the **Rollover Area** over the image of the number **1**

   ❑ resize the Rollover Area so that it just covers the image of number **1**

   The position of the Rollover Caption and Rollover Area should look similar to the picture below.

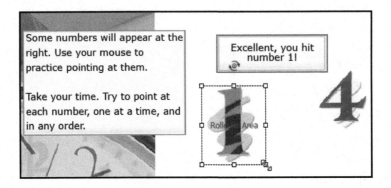

9. Save your work.

Rollover Captions Confidence Check

1. With the **Rollover area** selected, go to the **Timing Inspector** and change the **Appear After** time to **3 sec**.

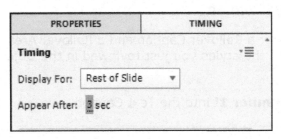

   On the Timeline, notice that the left edge of the Rollover Area now lines up with **00:03**. Why did I ask you to make the timing change? Take a further look at the Timeline. The four slide images appear on the slide at the 3-second mark. By delaying the availability of the Rollover Area, you have ensured that overanxious learners won't be able to use the Rollover Area and see the Rollover Caption until the images have appeared on the slide.

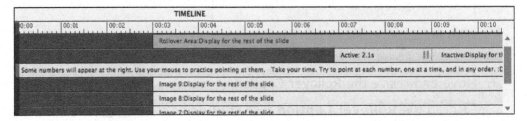

2. Preview the project.

3. After the numbers appear on slide 2, point to the number 1.

Your Rollover Caption should appear and disappear as you move your mouse over and then away from the number 1.

4. Close the preview.

5. Insert another Rollover Caption on slide 2 that looks like the picture below.

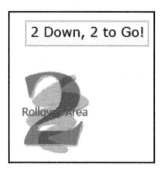

6. Insert another Rollover Caption that looks like the picture below.

7. Insert another Rollover Caption that looks like the picture below.

8. Change the timing for each of the new Rollover Areas so that they appear after **3** seconds (just like the first Rollover Area).

9. Preview the project and confirm that each Rollover Caption appears as expected.

10. When finished, close the preview and save your work.

Rollover Images

You learned about working with images beginning on page 84. Any image you can insert on a slide can instead be a Rollover Image. Similar to Rollover Captions, Rollover Images consist of an image and a rectangular "hot spot." Rollover Images appear in the published project only when the user moves the mouse over the hot spot. You might consider using Rollover Images within your projects as a way to offer enhanced views of a dialog box, tool, or schematic.

Student Activity: Insert a Rollover Image

1. Ensure that the **MouseSkills** project is still open.

2. Insert a Rollover Image onto a slide.

   ❑ go to slide **3**

   ❑ choose **Objects > Rollover Image**

   The Open dialog box appears. You can use several types of images as Rollover Images including jpeg, gif, bmp, emf, png, and pict.

   ❑ from the **Captivate9Data\images_animation** folder, open **mouse1.bmp**

   Two things appear on slide 3: the mouse image (which is the Rollover Image) and a Rollover Area. The Rollover Area is behind the mouse image. The two objects are shown pulled apart in the image below.

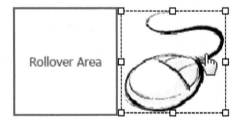

Rollover Images Confidence Check

1. Move both the Rollover Area and Rollover Image anywhere you'd like on the slide.

2. Insert a second Rollover Image that uses the **mouse2** image.

3. Insert a third Rollover Image that uses the **mouse3** image.

4. Preview the project and test the rollovers on slide **3**.

5. When finished, close the preview.

6. Save and close the project.

Rollover Slidelets

Rollover Slidelets are mini slides within a slide. Similar to Rollover Captions and Images, slidelets appear only when the user moves the mouse over a specified area on the slide. Unlike Rollover Captions (which can contain only text) and Rollover Images (which can contain only images), slidelets can contain images, text, audio, and video. In addition, you can attach navigation controls to a slidelet.

Student Activity: Insert a Rollover Slidelet

1. Open **RolloverSlideletMe** from the **Captivate9Data** folder.

   This project should look familiar to you. You worked with this project when you learned to create Text Captions (see page 66).

2. Insert a Rollover slidelet.

   ❑ go to slide **10** (the last slide)

   You're going to add a Rollover Slidelet on this slide. If learners click the **View** menu (indicated in the Text Caption), they see the menu items. If they don't care to click, they won't see the menu.

   ❑ choose **Objects > Rollover Slidelet**

   Two things appear on the slide: the **Rollover Slidelet Area** and the **Slidelet**. Although the two objects look similar, the Rollover Slidelet Area (which is smaller and the only one of the two objects containing descriptive text) serves as the interactive area. The Slidelet appears when the learner moves the mouse over the Rollover Slidelet Area (or clicks the area). Although the Rollover Slidelet Area contains the words "Rollover Slidelet Area," that text disappears as you make the Rollover Slidelet Area smaller.

   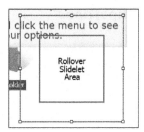

3. Move and resize the Rollover Slidelet Area.

   ❑ drag the **Rollover Slidelet Area** (the **smaller** of the two objects) over the **View** menu on the slide background; then resize it so that it is the same size as the **View** menu

4. Set the Slidelet to "Stick" if the Rollover Slidelet Area is clicked by the learner.

❏ with the resized and repositioned **Rollover Slidelet Area** still selected, go to the **Properties Inspector** and select the **Actions** tab

❏ select **Stick Slidelet**

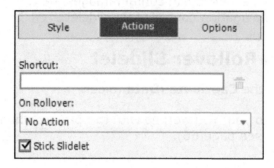

When the learner clicks the **Rollover Slidelet Area**, the **Stick Slidelet** option means the **Slidelet** continues to display for a few seconds, even when the learner moves the mouse away from the Rollover Slidelet Area. Alternatively, you could have selected from a list of On Rollover actions, such as **Jump to Slide** or **Open URL or File**.

5. Change the size and slide position of the Slidelet.

❏ select the **Slidelet** (the Slidelet is the larger of the two objects)

Note: Ensure you've selected the **Slidelet**, not the Rollover Slidelet Area. You are going to both resize the Slidelet and import an image into it. If you select with the Rollover Slidelet Area by mistake, you won't be able to insert the image.

❏ on the **Properties Inspector**, select the **Options** tab

❏ from the **Transform** area, deselect **Constrain proportions**

❏ change the **X** value to **83**

❏ change the **W** to **112**

❏ change the **Y** value to **79**

❏ change the **H** to **282**

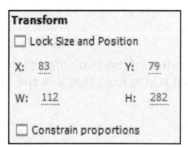

The Slidelet should be positioned just beneath the **View** menu. The size of the Slidelet matches the image you're about to import into the Slidelet.

6. Insert an image into the Slidelet.

   ❑ ensure that the **Slidelet** is still selected (again, the Slidelet is the larger of the two objects)

   ❑ choose **Media > Image**

   ❑ from the **Captivate9Data\images_animation** folder, open **ViewMenu.jpg**

   The image has been inserted within the Slidelet. If the Slidelet were larger, you would be able to move the image around the Slidelet, but you would be unable to drag it outside of the Slidelet.

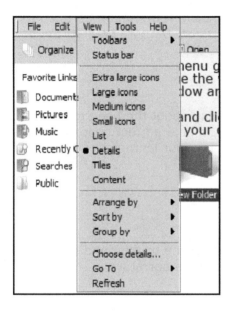

7. Preview From this slide.

   ❑ with slide **10** selected, choose **Preview > From this slide**

8. Click the Rollover Slidelet Area you positioned over the View menu.

   The Rollover Slidelet appears with the menu image you inserted. If you move your mouse away from the Rollover Slidelet Area, the Rollover Slidelet should stay for a few seconds and then disappear (this is the Stick behavior in action). Alternatively, you can point to the Rollover Slidelet Area. Using this technique, the menu image appears until you move your mouse away from the Rollover Slidelet Area.

9. Close the Preview.

10. Save your work and close the project.

Zoom Areas

You learned how Highlight Boxes can grab the learner's attention on page 119. Zoom Areas offer you an alternative method of grabbing the eye. Zoom Areas consist of two parts: the Zoom Source (the area you want to highlight on the screen) and the Zoom Destination (the enlarged view of the Zoom Area). During the next activity, you will use a Zoom Area to emphasize a specific tool in Adobe Photoshop.

Student Activity: Insert a Zoom Area

1. Open **PhotoshopVignette** from the **Captivate9Data** folder.

   This project was originally created by **Barbara Ash**, Adobe Certified Instructor and Captivate developer and design specialist. Barbara created the project to help her niece learn Adobe Photoshop.

2. Preview the project.

   Notice on slide **2** that the narrator is talking about the need to press and hold a tool on the toolbar at the left. This would be a perfect opportunity to use a Zoom Area to make the tool a bit larger for your learners.

3. Close the preview.

4. Go to slide **2**.

   You'll be adding the Zoom area at the left of the background (when the Rectangular Marquee Tool is mentioned by the narrator).

5. Insert a Zoom Area.

   ❏ still working on slide **2**, choose **Objects > Zoom Area**

   Two objects appear in the middle of the slide: the **Zoom Destination** and the **Zoom Source**. The appearance of these objects is controlled by Object Styles. As with the Rollover Captions you worked with earlier in this module, the Zoom styles have already formatted via the Object Style Manager.

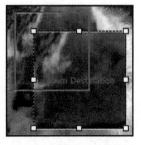

6. Reposition the Zoom Source and Zoom Destination.

    ☐ drag the **Zoom Source** over the **second tool in the toolbar at the left** (although the two objects look similar, look carefully at both, and you'll notice that the Zoom Source contains the words Zoom Source)

    ☐ resize the **Zoom Source** so that it is the same size as the tool

    ☐ drag the Zoom Destination below the menu shown to the right of the toolbar and resize it as shown in the image below

7. Set the Appear time for the Zoom Area to match the narration.

    ☐ select the **Zoom Source** (the first object you resized)

    ☐ on the Timing Inspector, change the **Appear After** to **2** sec

    Note: If you don't see a Timing Inspector, first ensure you've selected the Zoom Source, not the Zoom Destination. If you're sure you've selected the Zoom Source and there isn't a Timing Inspector, click the Properties icon in the upper right of the Captivate window to hide and then re-open the Inspectors.

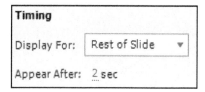

The narrator mentions the tool behind the Zoom Source at exactly two seconds. You've just set it up so that the zoom occurs as the tool is being discussed by the narrator.

8. Set the length of time for the zoom.

❒ ensure the Zoom Source is still selected

❒ on the Timing Inspector, change the **Zoom for** to **2** sec

> Appear After: 2 sec
>
> Zoom for: 2 sec

The **Zoom for** timing controls how long the zoom takes. You've just specified that the zoom take exactly two seconds.

9. Preview the lesson **From this slide**.

Notice that the tool mentioned by the narrator zooms out from the Zoom Source to the Zoom Destination.

10. Close the Preview.

11. Save your work and close the project.

iCONLOGiC

"Skills and Drills" Learning

Module 8: Audio

In This Module You Will Learn About:

And You Will Learn To:

Object Audio

You can import two types of audio files into a Captivate project: WAV and MP3. You can add audio to just about anything. During the activity that follows, you will import audio to some rollover captions and rollover images.

WAV (WAVE): WAV files are one of the original digital audio standards. Although high in quality, WAV files can be very large. In fact, typical WAV audio files can easily take up to *several megabytes of storage per minute* of playing time. If your learner has a slow Internet connection, the download time for large files is unacceptable.

MP3 (MPEG Audio Layer III): Developed in Germany by the Fraunhofer Institute, MP3 files are compressed digital audio files. File sizes in this format are typically 90 percent smaller than WAV files.

> **Note:** To learn more about digital audio formats, visit
> **www.webopedia.com/DidYouKnow/Computer_Science/2005/**
> **digital_audio_formats.asp**.

Student Activity: Import Audio onto a Slide Object

1. Open **AudioMe** from the **Captivate9Data** folder.

2. Add a sound effect to a Rollover Caption.

   ❐ go to slide **2** and select the **Excellent, you hit number 1!** caption

   ❐ choose **Audio > Import to > Object**

   The Import Audio dialog box opens. By default, you should be taken to the Sound folder that comes with Captivate. (If not, navigate to the folder where Captivate is installed (typically Program Files/Adobe/Adobe Captivate 9 on Windows; Applications/Adobe Captivate 9 on a Macintosh. Open the **Gallery** folder and then open the **Sound** folder.)

   ❐ open **Electronic Tink.mp3**

   The Object Audio dialog box opens.

3. Preview the sound.

   ❐ on the **Add/Replace** tab, click the **Play** button to hear the audio clip

   ❐ click the **Close** button

   The audio file is attached to the selected caption. At this point there is no way to know that the audio file has been attached to the object without previewing. You'll learn later that there is a dialog box called **Advanced Audio Management** that lets you see all of the audio files used in the project (and delete, export, update, and preview them).

Object Audio Confidence Check

1. Preview the project.

2. When you get to slide **2**, use your mouse to point to Image 1.

   The sound effect should play when the Rollover Caption appears.

3. Close the Preview.

4. Attach sounds to the remaining Rollover Captions on slide **2**.

   Note: You can use any of the sound files available in the **Sound** folder or the sound files in the **Captivate9Data\audio** folder. You will also find hundreds of free sound clips online at **http://www.grsites.com/sounds**.

5. Attach sounds to the Rollover Images on slide **3**.

6. Preview the project. There should be a sound effect attached to each Rollover Caption on slide **2** and to every Rollover Image on slide **3**.

7. When finished, close the preview.

Student Activity: Import Background Audio

1. Ensure that the **AudioMe** project is still open.

2. Import an audio file that plays for the entire project.

   ❑ choose **Audio > Import to > Background**

   ❑ from the **Captivate9Data**, **audio** folder, open **2Step1.mp3**

   The Background Audio dialog box opens.

   ❑ from the **Options** area of the **Add/Replace** tab, ensure that **Loop Audio** is selected

   The audio file you imported is large enough to play for just over one minute. By selecting Loop Audio, the music plays over and over. Using this technique, you can use smaller audio files for your background music.

   ❑ ensure that **Stop audio at end of project** is selected

   This option ensures that the background music stops when the project is closed by the learner.

   ❑ ensure that **Adjust background audio volume on slides with audio** is selected

   You'll soon be adding voice-over audio to slides 2 and 3. With **Adjust background audio volume on slides with audio** selected, the background music automatically lowers so that you'll be able to hear the voice-over audio without being distracted by the background audio.

   ❑ drag the slider at the right to **15%**

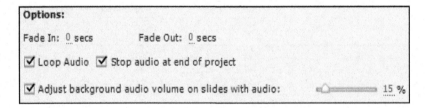

   When adjusting the background audio on slides with audio, the slider controls how much the background audio volume lowers. I've found that 15 percent works reasonably well in most circumstances.

   ❑ click the **Save** button and then click the **Close** button

3. Preview the project.

   You should be able to hear the background music, and when you get to the slides with the sound effects attached to objects, you should still be able to hear the sound effects along with the background audio. Because there isn't any voice-over audio on the slide yet, the volume of the background audio should not yet lower.

4. Close the preview, save, and close the project.

Slide Notes

Slide Notes can serve multiple functions. For instance, if you are working with a team of Captivate developers and sharing the Captivate projects, you can add Slide Notes that serve as production comments. If you elect to publish your project as a Word document (handouts), the Notes can be included and appear within the Word document. And because Slide Notes can be displayed when you record voice-overs in Captivate, you can use the Slide Notes as a digital narration script. During the next activity, you will use the Slide Notes feature to add a narration script that you will use when recording your voice (something you will do soon).

Student Activity: Add a Slide Note

1. Open **NarrateMe** from the **Captivate9Data** folder.

2. Open the Slide Notes panel.

   ☐ go to slide **2**

   ☐ choose **Window > Slide Notes**

   At the bottom of the Captivate window, there is now a **Slide Notes** panel where you can add Closed Captions, convert Text-to-Speech, and add Notes.

   ☐ at the far right of the Slide Notes panel, ensure **Notes** is selected from the drop-down menu

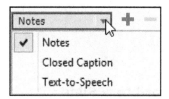

3. Add a slide Note.

   ☐ on the Notes panel, click in the space below the triangle at the left and type **Learning to use your mouse is a fundamental computer skill. Practice those skills now by pointing to the numbers that have appeared on this screen.**

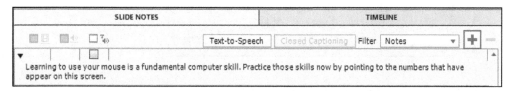

   During the next activity, you'll soon use the slide note as a narration script when you record voice-over audio.

Recording Audio

Captivate allows you to record and edit your own audio. There are three ways to work with sound files: you can attach audio to an entire lesson (running in the background), to an individual slide, or to any object on the slide. If you plan to record your own audio, you first need a microphone connected to your computer. Once you've got the microphone, consider the following:

Setup: If you plan to use high-end audio hardware, such as a mixer or preamplifier, plug your microphone into the hardware and then plug the hardware into your computer's "line in" port. Set the volume on your mixer or preamplifier to just under zero (this will minimize distortion).

Microphone placement: The microphone should be positioned four to six inches from your mouth to reduce the chance that nearby sounds are recorded. Ideally, you should position the microphone above your nose and point it down at your mouth. Also, if you position the microphone just to the side of your mouth, you can soften the sound of the letters *S* and *P*.

Microphone technique: It's a good idea to keep a glass of water close by and, just before recording, take a drink. To eliminate the annoying breathing and lip smack sounds, turn away from the microphone, take a deep breath, exhale, take another deep breath, open your mouth, turn back toward the microphone, and start speaking. Speak slowly. When recording for the first time, many people race through the content. Take your time.

Student Activity: Calibrate a Microphone

1. Ensure that the **NarrateMe** project is still open.

2. Select an Audio Input Device and Bitrate.

   ❏ still working on slide **2**, choose **Audio > Record to > Slide**

   The Slide Audio dialog box opens.

   ❏ at the top of the dialog box, click the link just below the word **Device**

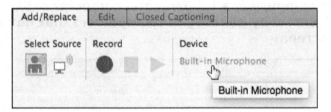

   The Audio Settings dialog box opens.

   ❏ from the **Audio Input Devices, Select** drop-down menu, select your computer's microphone (if you're not sure which device to select, try the one that says Built-In Microphone first)

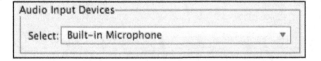

Note: If there are multiple microphones available in the Select drop-down menu, you'll be playing a game of trial and error. Make your best guess as to which selection to make. If you are unable to calibrate your microphone in the next few moments, return to this drop-down menu and try another microphone.

❏ from the Bitrate drop-down menu, ensure that **Constant Bitrate** is selected

Constant Bitrates lead to smaller, nice-sounding audio files. By contrast, Variable Bitrates tend to produce audio with a higher, consistent quality level, but the file sizes are larger than CBRs.

❏ if necessary, change the Encoding Bitrate to **FM Bitrate (64kbps)**

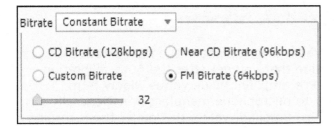

Using a higher Encoding Bitrate setting results in larger published lessons. If you decide to use a higher-quality bitrate than FM Bitrate, you should spend time experimenting with these options to see which selection sounds best. As a general rule, the FM Bitrate is more than adequate for audio that is played through typical computer speakers or headsets.

3. Calibrate the microphone.

❏ click the **Calibrate Input** button

```
Calibrate Input...
```

The **Calibrate audio input** dialog box opens. This is where you can set your microphone to its optimum recording level and sensitivity.

❏ click the **Auto calibrate** button

```
Auto calibrate
```

❏ speaking slowly and clearly, say

I am setting my microphone recording level for use with Adobe Captivate. While calibrating, it is important that I speak as normally as possible. What I do not want to do is talk either too loudly or too softly.

When the words **Input Level OK** appear beneath the meter at the right, you can stop speaking.

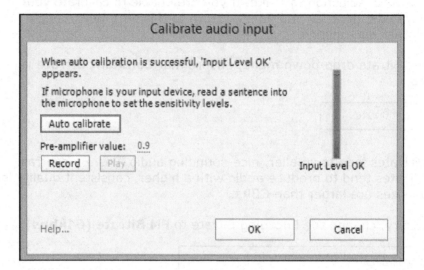

Note: The Pre-amplifier value that you see in the image above is probably not the same value that you get after the Auto calibration process is complete. The Pre-amplifier value varies widely from microphone manufacturer to microphone manufacturer. Generally speaking, the higher the Pre-amplifier value, the louder the recording volume.

❐ click each of the two **OK** buttons (one to close the Calibrate audio input dialog box and the other to close the Audio settings dialog box)

You should be back at the Slide Audio dialog box, ready to record your audio.

Student Activity: Record Slide Audio

1. Ensure that the **NarrateMe** project is still open. You should have also calibrated your microphone following the steps on page 144.

2. Practice the recording.

   ❒ click the **Captions & Slide Notes** button at the bottom of the dialog box

   The Note you created on page 143 opens in a dialog box.

   ❒ increase the size of the note text by clicking the increase size button (the larger of the two A's)

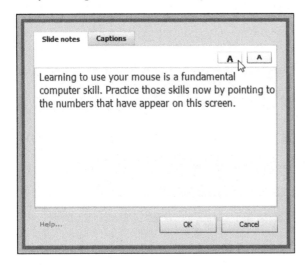

   ❒ take a deep breath and, using a not-too-fast cadence, read the slide Note out loud for practice:

   Learning to use your mouse is a fundamental computer skill. Practice those skills now by pointing to the numbers that have appeared on this screen.

3. Record a narration.

   ❒ from the **Select Source** area of the **Add/Replace** tab, ensure that Narration is selected

   Note: There is also a **System Audio** option in the **Select Source** area. When you select this option, Captivate records the sounds your computer makes while you record. This is especially helpful if you are recording a process on your computer that results in an alert tone. Using System audio, both your narration and the alert tone are recorded.

❏ click the **Record** button in the upper left of the slide Audio dialog box

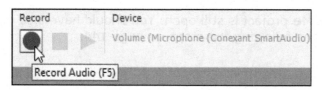

❏ after the countdown goes away, take your time and read the slide Note again: **Learning to use your mouse is a fundamental computer skill. Practice those skills now by pointing to the numbers that have appeared on this screen.**

❏ when finished, click the **Stop** button (located just to the right of the Record button)

❏ click the **OK** button to close the Caption and Slide Notes dialog box

Your recorded audio appears as a waveform.

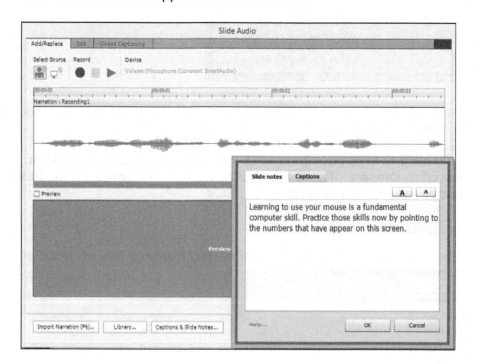

4. Preview the audio.

❏ click the **Play Audio** button, located to the right of the Stop button

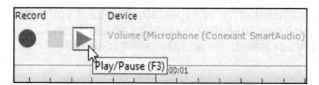

Recording Audio Confidence Check

1. If you are happy with the narration, click the **Save** button in the lower right of the dialog box and then click the **Close** button.

   If you are not happy with the audio and wish to rerecord, on the Add/Replace tab, click the **Record** button again and rerecord the audio. When finished, click the **Save** button and then click the **Close** button.

2. On the Filmstrip, notice that the thumbnail for slide 2 contains a tiny speaker icon, an indication that audio has been added to the slide.

3. Preview the project.

   Notice that when you get to slide 2, the background audio lowers automatically, and you can hear your narration.

4. Close the preview

5. Save and close the project.

Slide Audio

You've now learned that you can add audio to a slide object (page 140), add background audio to the entire project (page 142), and record your own audio (page 147). Now let's import audio directly to a slide.

Student Activity: Import Audio Onto a Slide

1. Open the **EditMyAudio** project from the **Captivate9Data** folder.

   This file is similar to the file you just closed, except it does not contain any slide audio or notes.

2. Import a prerecorded voice narration onto slide 2.

   ❏ go to slide **2** and then choose **Audio > Import to > Slide**

   ❏ from the **Captivate9Data\audio** folder, open **EditMyAudio.wav**

   Because the audio file you are importing plays longer than the slide, the **Audio Import Options** dialog box opens. You have three options: make the slide timing match the length of the imported audio, force the audio to play over multiple slides, or split the audio equally among all of the slides in the project.

   ❏ ensure **Show the slide for the same amount of time as the length of the audio file** is selected

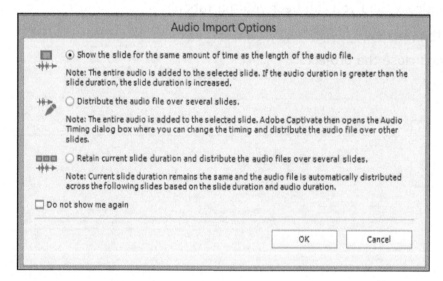

   ❏ click the **OK** button

   You can confirm that audio has been added to the slide via the **speaker icon** that appears in the lower right of the slide thumbnail on the Filmstrip.

3. Preview the imported slide audio.

   ❑ on the Filmstrip, click the audio icon on slide **2**

   ❑ choose **Play**

You should hear a bit of a problem with the imported slide audio. The narrator did not know the recording had begun, and you can hear a few gaffes and other background noises. To fix the problems, you can open the original audio file in an audio editing program (like Adobe Audition), edit and repair the issues, and then re-import the edited audio file into Captivate. Alternatively, you can use the audio editing features built within Captivate to edit the audio waveform without ever leaving Captivate. You will do that next.

Student Activity: Edit an Audio File

1. Ensure that the **EditMyAudio** project is still open and that you are on the second slide.

2. Edit an audio clip.

   ❑ still working on slide 2, choose **Audio > Edit > Slide**

   The Slide Audio dialog box opens. There are three tabs (Add/Replace, Edit, and Closed Captioning). You should be on the **Edit** tab.

3. Identify and select the problem areas of the waveform.

   ❑ from the top, center of the dialog box, drag the zoom slider **left** to zoom away from the waveform

   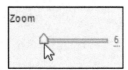

   Your goal is to delete the parts of the waveform that are bad while leaving the good parts alone. The best way to proceed is to select a single segment of the waveform, listen to it, ensure it's not something you want to keep, and then delete it.

   ❑ starting at the **far left** of the waveform, drag **right** to select the first **00:13** seconds of the audio (you can confirm you have selected 13 seconds worth of audio via the Selected area at the bottom right of the waveform)

   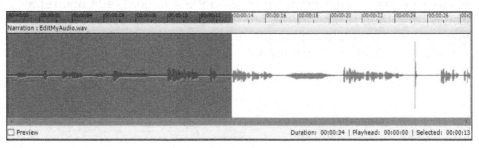

   ❑ click the **Play/Pause** button

   The selected 13 seconds of audio is junk and needs to be removed.

4. Delete the audio gaffe.

   ❑ click the **Delete** button

   And just like that, the selected portion of the audio is gone.

   ❑ click the **Play/Pause** button again to hear the remaining audio

   There are still some problem areas in the audio. However, with the first 13 seconds deleted, the remaining audio is much better.

   ❑ click the **Save** button and then click the **Close** button

Slide Audio Confidence Check

1. Edit the slide audio again. This time, delete the gaffe at the end of the waveform (the last few seconds where the narrator says she's glad the recording is over).

   There are a few more issues with this audio file, but you'll fix those later.

2. Click the **Save** button.

3. Click the **Close** button.

4. Go to slide **3**, and import the **MoveMousePointer.wav** audio to the slide.

5. Preview the project to hear the audio you've added to the project.

   The background audio is too loud, making it difficult to hear the narrator on slides 2 and 3. You'll fix that next.

6. Lower the background audio to something close to **5%** (**Audio > Edit > Background > Add/Replace** tab).

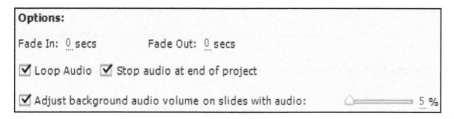

7. Preview the project again. Hopefully, this time the background music won't hinder the slide audio on slides 2 and 3. There are still a few issues with the slide audio, but you'll fix those soon enough.

8. Choose **Audio > Audio Management**.

   You can use the Audio Management dialog box to review the audio being used on every object on every slide, play the audio, and/or delete the audio.

9. Select **Show object level audio** (at the bottom left of the dialog box) to see a listing of every audio file used in the project.

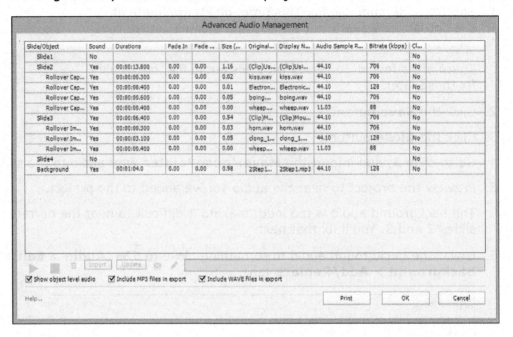

Slide/Object	Sound	Durations	Fade In	Fade ...	Size (...	Original...	Display N...	Audio Sample R...	Bitrate (kbps)	Cl...	
Slide1	No									No	
Slide2	Yes	00:00:13.800	0.00	0.00	1.16	(Clip)Us...	(Clip)Usi...	44.10	706	No	
Rollover Cap...	Yes	00:00:00.300	0.00	0.00	0.02	kiss.wav	kiss.wav	44.10	706	No	
Rollover Cap...	Yes	00:00:00.400	0.00	0.00	0.01	Electron...	Electronic...	44.10	128	No	
Rollover Cap...	Yes	00:00:00.600	0.00	0.00	0.05	boing....	boing.wav	44.10	706	No	
Rollover Cap...	Yes	00:00:00.400	0.00	0.00	0.00	wheep...	wheep.wav	11.03	88	No	
Slide3	Yes	00:00:06.400	0.00	0.00	0.54	(Clip)M...	(Clip)Mou...	44.10	706	No	
Rollover Im...	Yes	00:00:00.300	0.00	0.00	0.03	horn.wav	horn.wav	44.10	706	No	
Rollover Im...	Yes	00:00:03.100	0.00	0.00	0.05	clong_1...	clong_1...	44.10	128	No	
Rollover Im...	Yes	00:00:00.400	0.00	0.00	0.00	wheep...	wheep.wav	11.03	88	No	
Slide4	No									No	
Background	Yes	00:01:04.0	0.00	0.00	0.98	2Step1...	2Step1.mp3	44.10	128	No	

☑ Show object level audio   ☑ Include MP3 files in export   ☑ Include WAVE files in export

Help...   Print   OK   Cancel

10. Select any audio file you like and click the **Export** button at the bottom of the dialog box.

    You can now specify a folder and export any audio file from your project. This is an especially useful feature if you have recorded audio files directly in Captivate, have edited them, and then need to use them in other programs.

11. Cancel the export.

12. Cancel the Advanced Audio Management dialog box.

13. Save and close the project.

Silence

If you come across audio gaffes between waves in your waveform, it may not always be appropriate to delete them. Sometimes deleting parts of a waveform shortens the segments between two waves and has a negative effect on the timing for the rest of the audio. In those instances, it's a better idea to convert the gaffes into silence.

Student Activity: Insert Silence

1. Open **SilenceMe** from the **Captivate9Data** folder.

2. Go to slide **2** and open the Slide Audio dialog box. (**Audio > Edit > Slide**)

3. Click at the beginning of the waveform and then click the **Play/Pause** button.

   When you get to the 3-second mark, you can hear some pretty bad feedback.

4. Insert Silence.

   ❑ using your mouse, select the part of the waveform representing the feedback

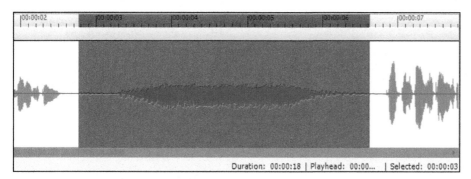

   ❑ at the top of the dialog box, click the **Insert Silence** command

   The audio feedback... gone!

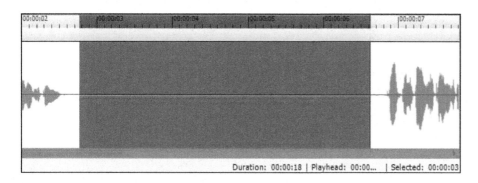

Edit Audio Confidence Check

1. There is a sharp "clap" sound near the 11-second mark. Replace it with silence.

   Now that you have replaced the "clap" sound with silence, return to where you earlier replaced the feedback noise with silence. There should be four full seconds of "dead air" near the 2-second mark on the waveform.

2. Highlight and delete approximately two-thirds of the "dead air" (leave one second of "dead air" so you leave a comfortable pause between the waves).

3. Edit the rest of the waveform and remove the remaining "dead air" so that there isn't more than one second of "dead air" between any segment.

4. Click the **Save** button, and click the **Close** button.

5. Preview the project.

6. When finished, save the project.

Text-to-Speech

Artificial voices have been around for years. In fact, there are many applications that allow you to select text and then have text-to-speech software convert the selected text into an audio file.

The problem with artificial voices used to be that the voices sounded artificial. Today's text-to-speech technology has made huge strides. Although not perfect, the text-to-speech voices sound more natural than ever before.

Why consider text-to-speech over recorded audio? If you record the audio yourself, you should budget several hours to record the audio and then to *clean* it up (remove lip smacks, other unwanted sounds, and static). In spite of your best efforts, the audio files you create might still be considered less than adequate. And consider the fact that your voice changes over the day. If you need to replace a small segment of a waveform, you will find it challenging to match the audio levels without sophisticated and expensive audio equipment. By using text-to-speech, you can ensure that the audio levels and quality are always consistent. And text-to-speech never gets sick, never takes a vacation, and never asks for compensation.

> **Note:** Before you can take full advantage of Captivate's text-to-speech voices, you need to install the NeoSpeech software. If you have not yet installed NeoSpeech, choose **Audio > Speech Management** and click the link at the bottom of the dialog box. The link takes you to a download page on Adobe's website.

Student Activity: Convert Text-to-Speech

1. Ensure that the **SilenceMe** project is still open.

2. Add Text-to-speech.

   ❏ choose **Audio > Speech Management**

   The Speech Management dialog box opens.

   ❏ select the **Slide 4** row

   ❏ click **Add Text-to-speech**

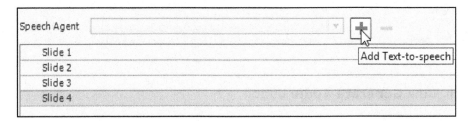

   ❏ type: **This concludes the lesson. Click the images on this screen to visit our website, send us email, or get social with us.**

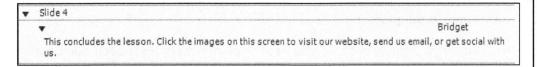

3. Select a Speech Agent.

    ❑ at the right of the Slide 4 row, select the current agent's name

    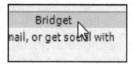

    Note: Depending on your computer platform and the text-to-speech agents installed on your computer, you may see a name other than Bridget.

    ❑ click the **Speech Agent** drop-down menu and choose any agent

    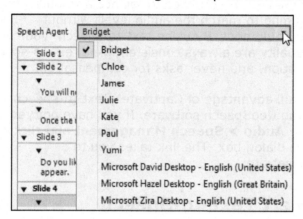

    Note: If you've installed NeoSpeech, Captivate comes with seven voices: Bridget, Chloe, James, Julie, Kate, Paul, and Yumi. Any other voices in your list were likely installed by some other application (or came with your computer). For instance, both Windows and the Mac OS include text-to-speech voices that serve as assistive devices for the visually impaired. The Macintosh comes with a bunch of voices including Hysterical and Zarvox (both are fun but not ideal Speech Agents). The NeoSpeech agents typically offer higher quality voices than those that ship standard on most computers.

    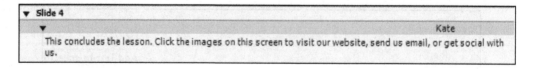

    ❑ click the **Generate Audio** button

    Generate Audio

    ❑ click the **Close** button

4. Preview the project.

    When you get to slide 4, you hear your new text-to-speech audio narration.

5. Save and close the project.

TTS Confidence Check

1. Open the **PhotoshopVignette** project from the **Captivate9Data** folder. (You first worked with this project beginning on page 136.)

2. Preview the project.

3. Notice that there is background audio playing throughout the project.

4. Notice that there is voice-over audio on most of the slides. The voice-over was created using the text-to-speech feature that you just learned how to use.

5. Close the project (no need to save if prompted).

6. Open the **AddAudioToMe** project from the **Captivate9Data** folder.

7. This project is identical to the **PhotoshopVignette** project—except there isn't any audio.

8. Import the **BeethovenSymphony9.mp3** audio to the background. (Need help? See page 142.)

9. Display the **Slide Notes** panel (Window menu).

10. Most of the slides include Slide Notes. Using any Speech Agent you like, use the text-to-speech feature to convert the notes on each slide to audio. (Need help? See page 157.)

    Note: Locate the **TTS check** box  in the **Slide Notes** panel on any slide. You can make quick work out of converting text to speech by clicking the TTS check box to select all of the notes on a slide. Do this for every slide throughout the project. After you've clicked the TTS check box, choose **Audio > Speech Management**. You can use this dialog box to quickly convert the slides notes to speech.

11. Save and close the project.

Notes

iCONLOGiC

"Skills and Drills" Learning

Module 9: Video, Animation, and Effects

In This Module You Will Learn About:

And You Will Learn To:

Video

You can add several types of video into a Captivate project, including AVI, MOV, and Flash Video (FLV or F4V). When importing the video, you can elect to import a file directly from your computer or from a web server, Flash Video Streaming Service, or Flash Media Server.

Student Activity: Insert a Flash Video

1. Open **AnimateMe** from the **Captivate9Data** folder.

2. Go to slide **1**.

   You will be adding a Flash Video to the left of the large logo.

3. Insert a Flash Video.

   ☐ choose **Media > Video**

   The Insert Video dialog box opens. You have two choices: Event Video (typically video that is expected to play on only one slide) and Multi-Slide Synchronized Video (video that is expected to play across multiple slides). Because the video you'll be working with is expected to play on only the first slide, you'll use Event Video.

   ☐ select **Event Video**

   ☐ from the **Where is your video file?** area, ensure that **On your Computer** is selected and then click the **Browse** button at the right

   ☐ navigate to **Captivate9Data\images_animation**

   ☐ open **welcomeToLesson.flv**

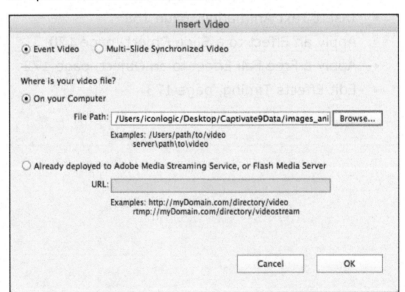

   ☐ click the **OK** button

   The video is imported, but it is so big it's covering the slide. You will resize the video next.

Student Activity: Set Flash Video Properties

1. Ensure that the **AnimateMe** project is still open.

2. Change the size of the video so it fits on the slide.

   ❏ with the video you just imported onto slide **1** selected, go to the **Properties Inspector**, **Options** tab

   ❏ from the **Transform** area, ensure **Constrain proportions** is selected

   ❏ change the **W** to **200** and then click in the **H** field

   Thanks to Constrain proportions, the Height of the video automatically changes to **150**.

   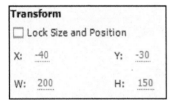

3. Change the slide location of the video.

   ❏ with the video still selected and still working on the **Transform** area, change the **X** to **152** and the **Y** to **128**

   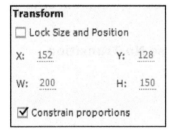

   Your slide 1 should look like the picture below.

4. Preview the Next 5 slides.

   A box where the video should play appears, but the video does not play. In addition, before you know it, the next slide appears. You'll fix both problems next.

5. Close the Preview.

6. Change the display timing and transition effect for the video.

   ❏ with the video on slide **1** still selected, select the **Timing Inspector**

   ❏ from the **Display For** drop-down menu, choose **Rest of Slide**

   ❏ ensure that **Pause slide till end of video** is selected

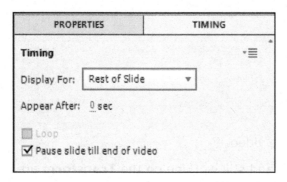

   The **Pause slide till end of video** option ensures that the first slide sticks around long enough for the video to play.

   ❏ from the **Transition** drop-down menu, choose **No Transition**

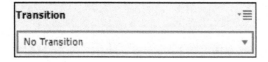

   Using Transitions is always optional. However, because they can cause partial fade in or fade out issues on slides with interactive objects (such as Buttons or Click Boxes), I tend to shy away from them unless they are adding value to the lesson.

7. Preview the Next 5 slides.

   This time the box containing the video appears, but the slide does not move on to slide 2 on its own.

8. On the video's Playbar, click the **Play** button to play the video.

   A guide walks onto the screen, introduces the lesson, and then exits, stage right.

9. Close the Preview.

   Next you will edit the Properties of the video to force the video to play on its own. You will also remove the video's playbar.

10. Remove the video's skin.

   ❐ with the video on slide **1** still selected, go to the **Properties Inspector** and select the **Style** tab

   ❐ from the **Skin** drop-down menu, choose **None**

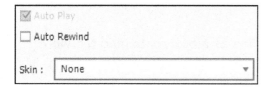

   On the **Properties Inspector**, notice that changing the **Skin** to **None** has also made **Auto Play** inactive, which will allow the video to play automatically when the lesson is previewed.

   ❐ on the **Properties Inspector**, select the **Options** tab

   ❐ from the **Transform** area, change the **X** value to **133** and ensure the **Y** value is **128**

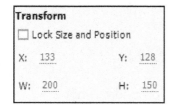

11. Preview the First 5 slides.

   Notice that the shell (the skin) surrounding the video has been removed, and the video plays automatically.

12. Close the Preview.

Animation

During the first activity in this module, you learned to import a video. But you can also import animations in either the Flash (SWF) or Animated GIF (GIF) format. If you have the time, software, and ability, you can create your own animations and import them into Captivate. You can also search the web for animations. However, if you go the web route, check for copyright restrictions on the animations you find. Captivate comes with several animations, which are in the **SWF Animation** folder (within the Captivate application **Gallery** folder).

Student Activity: Add Animation to a slide

1. Ensure that the **AnimateMe** project is still open.

2. Insert an animation.

   ❑ go to slide **2**

   ❑ choose **Media > Animation**

   You should automatically be browsing Captivate's SWF Animation folder. If not, navigate there now (typically, this is within Adobe > Adobe Captivate 9 > Gallery > SWF Animation).

   ❑ open the **Arrows** folder

   ❑ open the **Blue Fade** folder

   ❑ open **downright.swf**

   The animation shows up on your slide as a box containing the word "Animation."

   Next, you will change the animation's slide position and timing.

3. Save your work.

Animations Confidence Check

1. With the AnimateMe project still open, drag the Animation to the button at the right of the slide until the position of the Animation is similar to the image below.

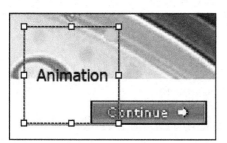

2. Preview the Next 5 slides and notice that the timing of the animation on slide 2 needs work. It would be better if the animation appears around the same time as the button (currently the animation appears right away, but the button does not appear until after 4 seconds).

3. Using the Timing Inspector, change the Display For time for the animation to **Rest of Slide**.

4. Change the Appear After to **4** sec.

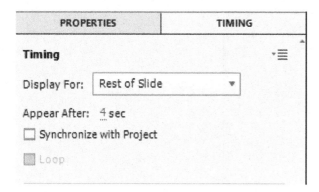

5. From the **Transition** area, change the Transition to **No Transition**.

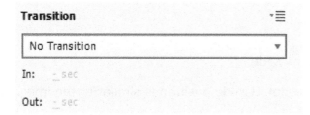

6. Preview the Next 5 slides and notice that the timing of the animation is now better.

7. Save your work (keep the project open for the next activity).

Text Animation

There are more than 90 Text Animations that come with Captivate. Although Text Animations are actually Flash objects, you don't have to own Flash or know how to use it to work with Text Animations. Text Animations are typically used to bring text to life. And although they are cool, I would recommend you use Text Animations sparingly because they can quickly become a distraction.

Student Activity: Insert Text Animation

1. Ensure that the **AnimateMe** project is still open.

2. On slide **2**, delete the **Creating New Folders** caption. (You're about to insert a text animation in its place.)

3. Insert Text Animation.

   ❑ still working on slide **2**, choose **Text > Text Animation**

   The Text Animation Properties dialog box appears.

   ❑ replace the words **Sample Text** with **Creating New Folders**

   ❑ change the **Font** to **Verdana** and the Size to **34**

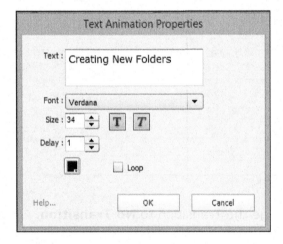

   ❑ click the **OK** button

   The animation appears on the slide.

   ❑ reposition the animation until its slide position is similar to the image below

4. Change animation effects.

❏ with the text animation selected, go to the Properties Inspector

❏ from the **Effect** drop-down menu, choose **Red_Hot_Skew**

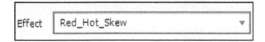

You see a sample of the effect at the top of the Properties Inspector.

❏ from the **Effect** drop-down menu, choose **Trailing_Light**

Once again, you see a sample of the effect in the area at the top of the Properties Inspector.

Text Animation Confidence Check

1. Using the Timing Inspector, change the **Display For** to **Rest of Slide** and the **Appear After** to **3** sec.

2. From the Transition area, change the Transition to **No Transition**.

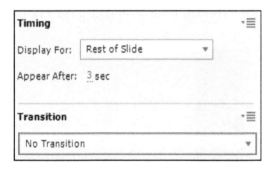

3. Preview the Next 5 slides to see the text animation in action. When finished, close the preview.

4. Save your work and then close the project.

Object Effects

You have now learned how to add videos (page 162), animation (page 166), and text animation (page 168) to your projects. But you can also apply effects to selected slide objects without ever leaving Captivate. You can right-click any slide object and choose Apply Effect. From there, you can use the Effects panel to add, remove, and control the timing of several effects that come with Captivate.

Student Activity: Apply an Effect to a Slide Object

1. Open **EffectMe** from the **Captivate9Data** folder.

2. Go to slide **2**.

   There are four text captions on the slide. You are about to apply two effects to the "During this demonstration..." caption.

3. Apply a Fly-In Effect to a Text Caption.

   ❒ select the text caption containing the words "During this demonstration..."

   ❒ on the **Timing Inspector**, **Effects** area, choose **Entrance** from the third drop-down menu

   ❒ from the bottom of the **Entrance Effects,** click **>** and choose **Fly in From Right**

On the **Timing Inspector**, the Effect has been added to the Applied Effects List. If you need to delete the Effect, you can click the **Trash** icon to the right of the Applied Effects List drop-down menu.

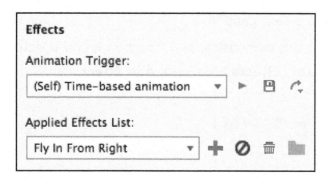

On the slide, notice that an FX has appeared in the upper right of the selected Text Caption. In addition, there's a red line starting on the Pasteboard and ending up on the caption.

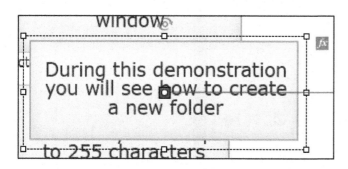

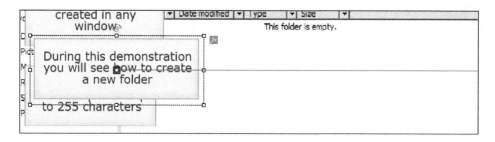

4. Preview the Next 5 slides.

   The text caption appears from the right side of the screen and stops in its original slide position.

5. Close the Preview and then save your work.

Student Activity: Apply a Free Fall Effect to an Object

1. Ensure that the **EffectMe** project is still open.

2. Apply a Emphasis Effect to a Text Caption.

   ❏ ensure that the "During this demonstration..." caption is still selected,

   ❏ on the **Timing Inspector**, **Effects** area, click **Add Effect**

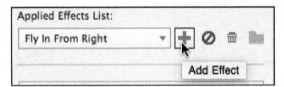

   ❏ from the **Effects** area, the third drop-down menu, choose **Emphasis**

   ❏ from the **Emphasis Effects**, choose **Free Fall**

3. Preview the Effects.

   ❏ choose **Preview > Play Slide**

   Both Effects work, but they occur at the same time. During the next activity you'll control the timing of both Effects.

Student Activity: Edit Effects Timing

1. Ensure that the **EffectMe** project is still open.

2. Change the timing for an Effect.

   ☐ on the **Timeline**, click the **arrow** to the **left** of the **During this demonstration** caption

   You can see the two Effects you've added to the caption.

   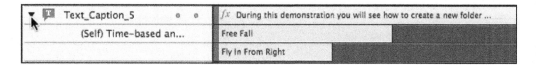

   ☐ drag the Free Fall effect right until its right edge lines up with the right edge of the **During this demonstration** caption

   ☐ drag the left edge of the Free Fall Effect a bit to the right (to shorten the playtime of the Effect similar to the image below)

   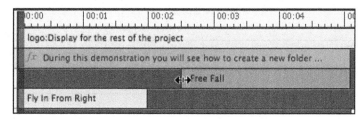

3. Save your work.

4. Play the Slide.

   The caption flies in from the right and stops. Then the Free Fall effect kicks in until the caption disappears off of the bottom of the slide.

5. Save your work and then close the project.

Notes

iCONLOGiC
"Skills and Drills" Learning

Module 10: Adding Interactivity

In This Module You Will Learn About:

And You Will Learn To:

Demonstrations versus Simulations

The three most common types of eLearning lessons that developers create with Captivate are soft skills training, software demonstrations, and software simulations. At the beginning of this book, you learned how to create a soft skills lesson from scratch (page 24). You then learned how to record actions and create software demonstrations and interactive simulations (beginning on page 46).

For the bulk of this book, I have focused on creating and cleaning up demonstrations—projects that are intended to demonstrate actions taken on a computer. Although you added some interactivity to a project when you learned about buttons (page 32), the projects have not encouraged user interaction. Learners watching a demonstration would be expected to merely sit back and watch slide objects appear on the screen and watch the mouse move around the slide. Although there is nothing wrong with demonstrations, simulations can improve the learning experience by letting users actively participate in the lesson.

Most people who teach themselves Captivate create demonstrations. Why? The most common reasons I hear are (1) I didn't know how to create a simulation and (2) I thought creating a simulation would be too hard. After this module, you will know how to quickly take an existing demonstration and convert it into a simulation. I'm hoping you will agree that simulations are not difficult to create.

Student Activity: Hide the Mouse

1. Open **ConvertMeToSimulation** from the **Captivate9Data** folder.

   On the Filmstrip, notice that there is a mouse icon  in the lower right of slides **3** through **9**. The mouse icon is a visual indicator that the mouse pointer is appearing on the slide. This demonstration project has been saved with a new name so that it can be converted into a simulation. One step to converting a demonstration into a simulation is to hide the mouse.

2. Hide the mouse for slides 3 through 9.

   ❑ on the **Filmstrip**, select slides **3** through **9**

   Note: One way to select the range of slides is to select slide **3**, press [**Shift**] on your keyboard, and then click one time on slide **9**.

   ❑ choose **Modify > Mouse > Show Mouse** (to turn the Show Mouse command off)

   The image at the left shows slide 3 with the mouse icon in the lower right of the slide thumbnail. The second image is missing the mouse icon.

Find and Replace

Although you can use Captivate's Find and Replace feature to find any object in your project (including images, animation, and Flash video), this feature is most useful for quickly replacing words or phrases throughout a project. During the following activity, you will use Captivate's Find and Replace feature to replace phrases to make the lesson more action oriented.

Student Activity: Replace Phrases

1. Ensure that the ConvertMeToSimulation project is still open.

2. Go to slide **3**.

   Notice that the text in the Text Caption (**Watch as the File menu is selected**) as written does not encourage the learner to interact with the lesson. The learner is being encouraged to simply "watch" as something happens. You'll use the Find and Replace feature to replace the phrase "Watch as" with "Select."

3. Replace a phrase.

   ☐ choose **Edit > Find and Replace**

   The Find and Replace panel opens.

   ☐ from the **Search In** drop-down menu, select **Text Caption** (if necessary)
   ☐ from the **Style** drop-down menu, ensure that **All Styles** is selected
   ☐ in the **Find** field, type **Watch as**
   ☐ in the **Replace** field, type **Select**
   ☐ from the lower left of the panel select **Match Case**

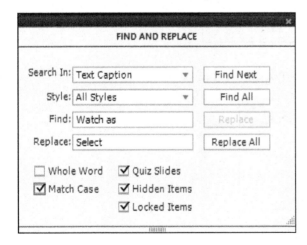

   Ensure that you typed both entries exactly as written above and have matched the case.

   ☐ click the **Find Next** button

   The first caption containing the phrase you typed into the Find field is selected.

❏ click the **Replace All** button

You are alerted that four instances of the phrase have been found and replaced.

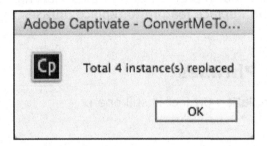

❏ click the **OK** button

Find and Replace Confidence Check

1. Use the Find and Replace feature to delete the phrase **is selected** from all of the Text Captions.

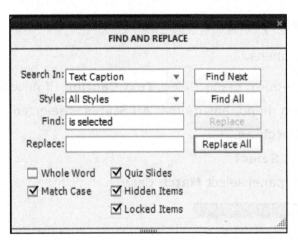

You should be alerted of four more changes to the project.

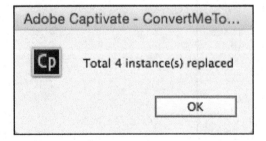

2. Close the Find and Replace panel.

3. Save your work.

Click Boxes

Instead of telling and then showing a learner how to perform an action, you can insert Click Boxes that allow the learner to perform actions, such as clicking a menu or menu command.

Student Activity: Insert a Click Box

1. Ensure that the **ConvertMeToSimulation** project is still open.

2. Preview the project.

   There is an interactive button on the first slide. Clicking the button takes you to slide 2. From this point forward, there is no interactivity in the project.

3. Close the preview.

4. Insert a Click Box on slide **3**.

   ☐ go to slide **3**

   ☐ choose **Interactions > Click Box**

   A new Click Box appears in the middle of your screen. The mouse badge on the lower right of the Click Box, although small, contains valuable information. If you look closely, you see a green icon on the top left side of the mouse badge indicating that the Click Box is activated with a left click. You can use the Click Box Properties to set the box to be right clickable by your learners, in which case the right side of the mouse badge is green.

   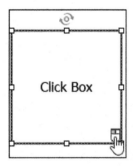

5. Confirm the On Success action and Attempts settings for the Click Box.

   ☐ double-click the newly inserted Click Box

   ☐ on the **Properties Inspector**, select the **Actions** tab

   ☐ from the **On Success** drop-down menu, ensure **Go to the next slide** is selected

   Using this Action, the learner immediately is taken to slide 4 when the Click Box is clicked.

   ☐ ensure that **Infinite Attempts** is selected

Using this option, a learner can click outside of the Click Box again and again. However, the **Go to the next slide** action does not occur until the learner successfully clicks the Click Box.

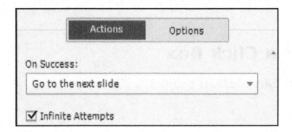

6. Add a Failure Caption to the Click Box.

❑ still working on the **Properties Inspector**, **Display** area, select **Failure**

A Failure caption appears on the slide along with the Click Box. This is what learners see when they click anywhere on the slide except the Click Box.

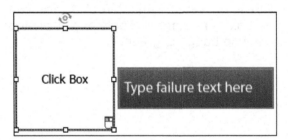

Note: The **Pause for Success/Failure Captions** option you see in the **Others** area ensures that the learner is given a chance to read the Failure Caption before getting frustrated and clicking again in the wrong place. The **Disable Click Sound** option ensures that the learners don't hear a double-click sound when they click the Click Box (their click and one created by the Click Box). And **Pause project until user clicks** ensures that the lesson does not continue unless the learner interacts with the Click Box.

7. Reposition the Click Box.

❑ **drag** the Click Box **up** and to the **left** and resize it so that it covers the word "File" in the File menu on the slide background

8. Position the Failure Caption on the slide.

   ❏ position the Failure Caption to the right of the Click Box

9. Edit the Failure Caption's text.

   ❏ right-click the Failure Caption and choose **Edit Text**

   ❏ replace the text with **Ooops. You need to select the File menu.**

10. Your screen should look similar to the image below.

Click Boxes Confidence Check

1. Preview the project from slide 3.

2. Test the Failure Caption by clicking anywhere except the File menu.

3. Close the Preview.

4. Go to slide **5**.

5. Insert a Click Box over the **New** command on the slide. The Click Box should take learners to the **next slide** when they click it.

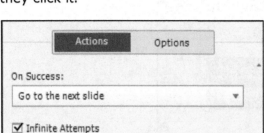

6. Edit the Failure Caption text so that it reads **Sorry but you need to select the New Command**.

7. Position the Click Box over the New command and then resize the Click Box as necessary so it is no larger than the **New** command.

8. Position the Failure Caption so it is similar to the picture below.

9. Insert similar Click Boxes on slides **6** and **8**. (The exact wording you use in the Failure captions is up to you.)

10. When finished, preview the project and test each of the Click Boxes you added.

11. Close the preview.

12. Save and close the project.

Text Entry Boxes

You can use Text Entry Boxes to simulate areas in an application that require a user to type data. Learners can be instructed to type specific information into a Text Entry Box and, depending on what they type, captions can provide the appropriate feedback.

Student Activity: Insert a Text Entry Box

1. Open **PasswordMe** from the **Captivate9Data** folder.

2. On slide 1, notice that there is a Text Caption instructing the learner to enter a password to take the course. You will create a Text Entry Box that accepts a specific password.

3. Insert a Text Entry Box.

   ☐ choose **Text > Text Entry Box**

   Two objects appear on the slide: a Text Entry Box and a submit button. As with most objects, the appearance of objects is controlled by Object Styles. I have already edited the Object Styles via the Object Style Manager.

   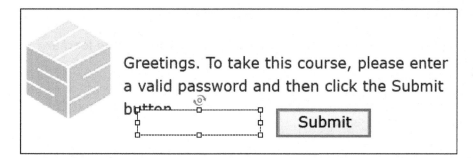

4. Validate User Input.

   ☐ double-click the **Text Entry Box**

   ☐ on the **Properties Inspector**, **Style** tab, select **Validate User Input**

   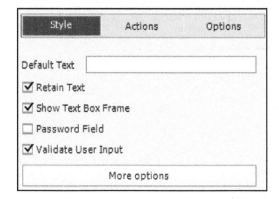

   A **Correct Entries** dialog box appears on the slide. You can now set it up so that there are correct answers associated with the Text Entry Box.

❏ in the upper right of the **Correct Entries** dialog box, click the **Plus** sign

❏ type **captivate** as the Correct Entry

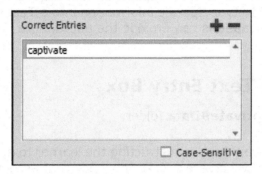

5. Set more Properties for the Text Entry Box.

❏ ensure the Text Entry Box is still selected

❏ on the **Properties Inspector**, **Style** tab, deselect **Retain Text**

With this option deselected, the text a learner types into the Text Entry Box is removed when the learner chooses to rewind and work through the lesson again.

❏ if necessary, select **Show Text Box Frame**

This option ensures that the Text Entry Box is visible to the learner.

❏ select **Password Field**

With this option selected, the text a learner types into the Text Entry Box is replaced with asterisks.

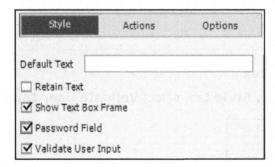

6. Set the Action for the Text Entry Box.

   ❏ ensure the Text Entry Box is still selected

   ❏ select the Actions tab on the Properties Inspector

   ❏ from the On Success drop-down menu, choose **Go to the next slide**

   ❏ ensure that **Infinite Attempts** is selected

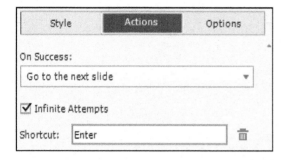

7. Enable a Failure caption.

   ❏ from the Display area, select **Failure**

Text Entry Box Confidence Check

1. Move/resize/edit the screen objects until the slide looks similar to the image below.

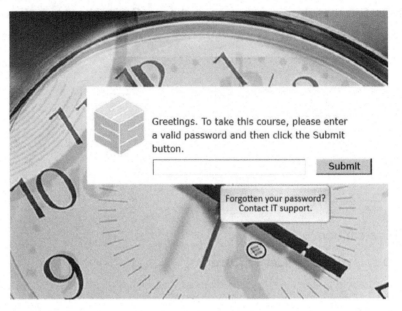

2. Preview the Next 5 slides.

3. Type **Hello** into the Text Entry Box on slide **1** and then click the **Submit** button.

   Because you did not type the text correctly, the Failure Caption appears.

4. Type **captivate** into the box and then click the **Submit** button.

   This time the lesson should continue without incident.

5. Close the preview.

6. Save and close the project.

Module 11: Working With PowerPoint

In This Module You Will Learn About:

- Starting with PowerPoint, page 188
- PowerPoint Collaboration, page 195
- Rescaling Projects, page 197

And You Will Learn To:

- Import a Presentation, page 188
- Apply Changes to All Items, page 192
- Edit the Presentation, page 193
- Synchronize With Source, page 195
- Rescale a Project, page 197

Starting with PowerPoint

If you or an SME has already created a presentation using Microsoft PowerPoint, don't throw it away. You can import the presentation slides into an existing Captivate project or create a new project that uses the PowerPoint slides. During the import process, Captivate creates a link between the Captivate project and the original PowerPoint presentation. Using this workflow, most changes made to the original PowerPoint presentation can be reflected in the Captivate project.

> **Note:** Microsoft PowerPoint must be installed on your computer before you can import PowerPoint presentations into Captivate. Additionally, you should not work within PowerPoint while a presentation is being imported into Captivate.

Student Activity: Import a Presentation

1. Create a new project from a PowerPoint presentation.

   ☐ choose **File > New Project > Project From MS PowerPoint**

   The Open dialog box appears.

   ☐ from the **Captivate9Data** folder, open **S3_Policies.pptx**

   > **Note:** If you are using an old version of PowerPoint (version 2003 or older), try to open S3_Policies. If you get an error message, open **S3_Policies_For_PowerPoint2003AndOlder** instead.

   The **Convert Microsoft PowerPoint Presentations** dialog box opens, offering a few controls over the way the PowerPoint presentation will be imported into Captivate.

   ☐ if the current Width and Height isn't 800 x 600, click the **Preset Sizes** menu and choose **800 x 600**

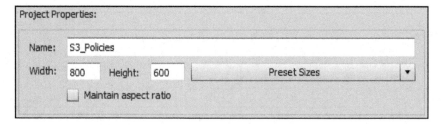

The presentation consists of only 10 slides. The slides contain hyperlinks created in PowerPoint that continue to work once the import process into Captivate is complete. Audio and transition settings are other popular PowerPoint features that import nicely into Captivate.

2. Set the PowerPoint to Captivate conversion options.

❏ ensure that **Selected slides: 10/10** appears at the bottom of the dialog box (if not, click the **Select All** button)

❏ from the **Advance Slide** drop-down menu, ensure **On mouse click** is selected

The **On mouse click** option adds a large click box to each slide in the pending Captivate project. The other available option, **Automatically**, results in Captivate slides that continue from slide to slide after a delay of just a few seconds. Between the two options, **On mouse click** is the more common and results in a more interactive eLearning lesson in Captivate.

❏ Windows users, select **High Fidelity** (the option is not available for Mac users)

During a standard import process, PowerPoint pptx presentations are first converted to the ppt format and then converted to SWF. If you select **High Fidelity**, the import process takes native pptx files directly to Captivate SWF (the ppt conversion is skipped). This option, which is available only in Captivate for Windows, results in the best-looking content in Captivate, but it could take a long time to import. (Five minutes or more in some cases.)

❏ all users, ensure **Linked** is selected

Linked creates a link between the PowerPoint presentation and the new Captivate project. The link allows you to open the PowerPoint presentation from within Captivate. Additionally, any changes made externally to the PowerPoint presentation can be reflected in the Captivate project with a few simple mouse clicks.

❏ click the **OK** button

When you change the size of the imported presentation to 800 x 600 (typically it's the Mac users who need to do so), you'll get an alert dialog box that's concerned with the resolution of the resulting Captivate project. If you had changed the size of the project to something larger than the original, resolution might be negatively affected. In this instance, there isn't anything to worry about, so you can click the **Yes** button.

After you click the OK button, the presentation is imported into Adobe Captivate and the PowerPoint slides are added to Captivate's Filmstrip.

Be patient. The import process can take several minutes (even if you hadn't selected High Fidelity), and you will likely see PowerPoint start and possibly come to the front of the Captivate interface.

During my tests, it took just over five minutes and the dreaded "Not Responding" message appeared multiple times, both within the alert box and for Adobe Captivate itself. Although slow, the process completed every time.

Once the presentation is imported, the Adding Microsoft PowerPoint Slides alert appears. This process completes relatively quickly.

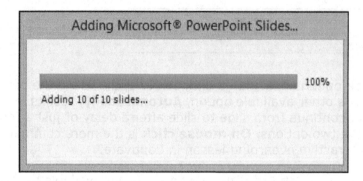

Once the import process completes, you will end up with a new 10-slide Captivate project (one Captivate slide for every PowerPoint slide).

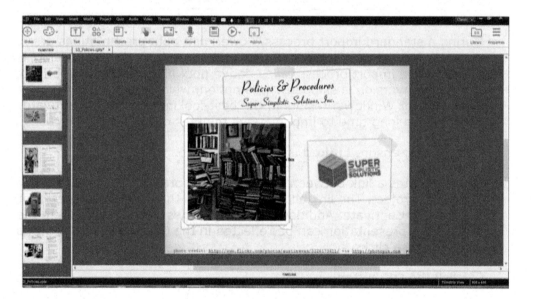

3. Save the project to the **Captivate9Data** folder as **S3_Policies_Integration**.

4. Preview the project.

   ❑ choose **Preview > Project**

Because a click box has been added to each of the Captivate slides during the import process, you will need to click your mouse once on each slide to move through the presentation. As I mentioned earlier, I've found that every aspect of PowerPoint that I've tested (hyperlinks, audio, transitions, and animations) continues to work as a Captivate project. I haven't tested everything. If you happen upon a PowerPoint feature that does not work within Captivate, please let me know (email me at ksiegel@iconlogic.com).

5. Test the hyperlinks that were created in PowerPoint.

   ❏ as you move through the presentation, click any of the links you see at the bottom of the slides

   You should notice some peculiar behavior as you attempt to click the links. Did each click successfully take you to the websites indicated in the link? Or did your click take you to the next slide? Or maybe you experienced both behaviors as you moved from slide to slide.

   What's up with the often contradictory behavior? There is a large Click Box on each slide that covers the entire slide. The default timing for every Click Box is keeping the Click Box from being active on the slide for the first few seconds of playtime. During the preview, if you clicked the web link right away, you were taken online to the target of each link. If you were a bit slower, your click actually didn't click the web link at all. Instead, your click was actually on the Click Box, which is so big that it is covering the web links on each slide. You'll fix the problem next by resizing all of the click boxes in the project.

6. Close the preview (keep the **S3_Policies_Integration** project open).

Student Activity: Apply Changes to All Items

1. Ensure that the **S3_Policies_Integration** project is still open.

2. Resize a single click box.

   ❑ go to any slide in the project and double-click in the middle of the slide (not the thumbnail of the slide on the Filmstrip, but the slide itself)

   Because the click box is as big as each slide (800 x 600), clicking the middle of the slide actually selects the click box, not the slide background.

   ❑ on the **Properties Inspector**, select the **Options** tab

   ❑ from the **Transform** area, remove the check mark from **Constrain proportions**

   You're about to change the height of the click box. If you hadn't deselected Constrain proportions, changing the height of the click box would also inadvertently change the width of the click box.

   ❑ change the **H** value from 600 to **550**

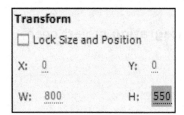

   The selected click box should now be short enough that it is no longer covering the link on the slide background. However, when you go to a different slide, you notice that none of the click boxes on any of the other slides have transformed.

3. Apply the new height to all of the click boxes in the project.

   ❑ with the click box that you just transformed still selected return to the **Transform** area of the **Properties Inspector**

   ❑ from the **far right** of the **Transform** area, click the menu and choose **Apply to all items of this type**

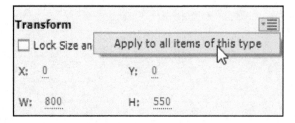

4. Go from slide to slide and check the click boxes throughout the project.

   Thanks to **Apply to all items of this type**, every click box in the project has resized to 550 pixels. The hyperlinks at the bottom of each slide are now accessible when you preview the project.

Student Activity: Edit the Presentation

1. Ensure that the **S3_Policies_Integration** Captivate project is still open.

2. Edit the slides with PowerPoint.

   ❑ choose **Edit > Edit with Microsoft PowerPoint > Edit Presentation**

   The Captivate slides that originated in PowerPoint open in the original PowerPoint presentation. If you've used PowerPoint before, you recognize the familiar PowerPoint interface. However, if you are using Windows, there are two buttons you wouldn't normally see in PowerPoint: the **Save** and **Cancel** buttons at the upper left of the window. (Although the Save and Cancel buttons do not exist for Mac users, the editing process works just fine.)

   ❑ go to slide **2** of the PowerPoint presentation

   ❑ at the right of slide 2, delete the words "for file collaboration, shared access and website management" and replace them with **in the world.** (The text should now read: **To continually develop the finest file management software in the world.**)

3. Save the PowerPoint changes and update the Captivate project.

   ❑ Windows users, click the **Save** button in the upper left of the window; Mac users, quit PowerPoint (save when prompted)

   Windows users, the changes you just made to the PowerPoint presentation are saved, the PowerPoint presentation is closed, and the Captivate slides are automatically updated in Captivate. Mac users, you are prompted to import the updated presentation (which you should allow by clicking the **Yes** button).

4. Preview the Captivate project.

   You can now click any of the links on the bottom of any of the slides. In addition, the edit made to the second slide in PowerPoint has made its way into the Captivate project.

5. Close the preview (keep the project open).

Apply to All Confidence Check

As mentioned earlier, there is a large click box on every Captivate slide (thanks to the **On Mouse Click** option you selected during the import process you went through on page 188). The click boxes are great because they keep the lesson from moving forward until the learner clicks the click box. However, the click box includes what is often considered an annoying click sound. You'll remove that next.

1. Double-click the middle of any slide to select the slide's click box.

2. From the **Actions** tab on the **Properties Inspector**, **Others** area, select **Disable Click Sound**.

3. Use the menu at the right of the **Display** area to apply your change to **all items of this type**.

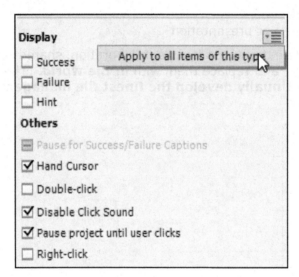

4. Save your work.

5. Preview the project and notice that the click sound has been removed.

6. Close the preview (keep the project open).

PowerPoint Collaboration

You have just learned that as a Captivate developer, you can import a PowerPoint presentation and, thanks to the Link feature, initiate changes to the PowerPoint presentation from within Captivate. *Nice!* But let's assume that you've imported the presentation from a network drive. An SME has made changes to the original PowerPoint presentation but has neglected to tell you. If the source PowerPoint presentation is updated, you are able to see that the Captivate project is no longer synchronized with the PowerPoint presentation via the Library, and you can grab the updates.

Student Activity: Synchronize With Source

1. Minimize (Hide) Captivate, and open the **S3_Policies** presentation directly in PowerPoint.

2. Edit the slides with PowerPoint.

   ❏ using PowerPoint, open the **S3_Policies** presentation (the presentation is in the **Captivate9Data** folder)

   Note: If you used the **S3_Policies_For_PowerPoint2003AndOlder** PowerPoint presentation when you started this module, open it now instead of S3_Polcies.

   ❏ go to slide **3**

   ❏ at the top of the Alcohol text box, add the phrase **Alcohol is** in front of the phrase **Not permitted** and then lowercase the "n" in **Not**

   ```
   Alcohol

   Alcohol is not permitted on
   company property.

   Failure to comply will result
   in disciplinary action.
   ```

3. Save the presentation and exit (quit) PowerPoint.

4. Return to Captivate. (The **S3_Policies_Integration** project should still be open.)

5. Go to slide 3 of the Captivate project.

   Notice that the edits made externally to the PowerPoint presentation do not appear on the slide. You'll update the Captivate project with the changes you made in the PowerPoint presentation next.

6. Open the Library.

❏ at the far right of the Captivate window, click **Library**

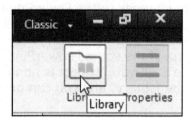

On the Library, notice that there is a **Status** column (you may need to resize the Library to see the Status column). The red button indicates that the S3_Policies presentation within the Captivate project is no longer synchronized with the PowerPoint presentation. (The changes you just made to the presentation have not yet been reflected in the Captivate project.)

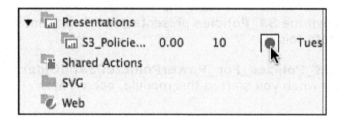

7. Synchronize with source.

❏ click the **Red** button

The edited PowerPoint slides are updated in the Captivate project. On the Library, the color of the button in the Status column changes from red to green.

Note: Be patient as the update process progresses. Depending on the speed of your computer, the process could take a few moments.

❏ go to slide 3 of the Captivate project

Notice that the edits you made in the PowerPoint presentation appear on the Captivate slide.

8. Save your work.

Note: If you no longer want the PowerPoint presentation in your project to be linked to the original PowerPoint presentation, you can **embed** the presentation in your project. On the Library, right-click the presentation and choose **Change to Embedded**. Once embedded, the size of your Captivate project increases significantly and you are no longer able to receive updates from the original PowerPoint presentation. If you change your mind, you can restore the link to the original presentation by right-clicking the presentation on the Library and choosing **Change to Linked**.

Rescaling Projects

If your project was recorded at a specific size and you now need it to be bigger or smaller, you can use Captivate's **Rescale project** command to quickly resize it—a real time saver over having to rerecord the entire lesson. When you rescale the project, you can instruct Captivate to ensure that the project's captions are rescaled if the resized project is smaller than the original.

> **Note:** You will not be able to use the Undo command to undo a rescale. Also, if you rescale a project, you could degrade the visual quality of the project.

Student Activity: Rescale a Project

1. Ensure that the **S3_Policies_Integration** project is still open.

2. Rename the project.

   ☐ choose **File > Save As**, change the name to **S3_Policies_Integration_Resized**, and save it to the **Captivate9Data** folder

3. Rescale a project larger.

   ☐ choose **Modify > Rescale project**

   The Rescale Project dialog box appears.

   ☐ in the **Size** area, ensure that **Maintain Aspect Ratio** is selected

   ☐ change the **Width** to **1200** and press [**tab**]

   Once you leave the Width field, the Height should automatically become **900** (thanks to the **Maintain Aspect Ratio** option).

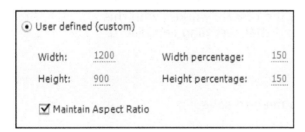

   ☐ from the **If new size is larger** area, select **Rescale Project to Fit New Size** (if necessary)

   ☐ ensure that **Rescale all Objects** is selected

Although just about everything in the project comes directly from the PowerPoint presentation, there are click boxes on every slide. Thanks to the Rescale options, each of those click boxes is going to resize proportionally to the new size of the project.

❏ click the **Finish** button

A warning appears. As mentioned earlier, you cannot undo this step. However, if you are not satisfied with the results, you can close the project without saving.

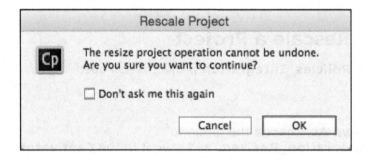

❏ click the **OK** button

The project's slides are now much larger.

Rescaling Confidence Check

1. Preview the project.

2. As you move from slide to slide, notice that the quality of the slides is actually quite good (astonishing, considering that you rescaled the project to make it significantly larger).

   Note: Although the quality of the rescale worked with this particular project, keep in mind that rescaling can lead to a loss of image quality.

3. Close the preview.

4. Close the project (there is no need to save it).

iCONLOGiC

"Skills and Drills" Learning

Module 12: Introduction to Question Slides

In This Module You Will Learn About:

And You Will Learn To:

Quiz Setup

You will soon be adding a few question slides to an existing Captivate project. Before proceeding, it's a good idea to set up a few things that will make the process of creating a quiz a bit more efficient. For instance, if you set up the Object Styles for the Quiz objects, the question slides will look consistent throughout the project. In addition, you should set some basic Quiz Preferences to control such things as general quiz navigation and the Pass/Fail options.

Student Activity: Edit Quizzing Object Styles

1. Open **QuizMe** from the **Captivate9Data** folder.

2. Use the Object Style Manager to set the formatting for Quizzing Objects.

   ❑ choose **Edit > Object Style Manager**

   ❑ at the upper left of the Object Style Manager dialog box, expand the **Quizzing Objects**

   ❑ expand the **Captions**

   ❑ from the list of captions, select **Correct Caption**

   ❑ at the right side of the dialog box, from the **Text Format** area, change the **Family** to **Trebuchet MS**

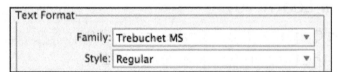

3. Review some of the other Quizzing Object styles.

   ❑ from the **Quizzing Objects** area, select any of the remaining objects

   ❑ spend a few minutes observing the Caption Type, Text Format, and Transition settings for the styles

   The project is using a Theme and the settings, along with the formatting of some of the slides, are based on that Theme.

   ❑ click the **OK** button

Student Activity: Set the Quiz Preferences

1. Ensure that the **QuizMe** project is still open.

2. Set the Quiz Preferences.

    ☐ choose **Quiz > Quiz Preferences**

    The Preferences dialog box opens.

    ☐ from the **Quiz** category at the left, select **Settings**

    ☐ from the **Quiz** area, change the Name of the Quiz to **Folders Quiz**

    ☐ from the Required drop-down menu, select **Answer All - The user must answer every question to continue**

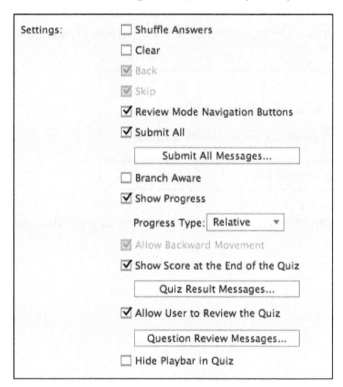

    ☐ from the **Settings** area, ensure your options match the picture below

After a learner answers a question in the quiz, the learner needs to be diligent about clicking the slide's Submit button before going to the next question. Failure to click the Submit button means that Captivate treats the answer as incorrect, even if the learner selects the correct answer. To prevent learners from accidentally failing to click the Submit button and causing a lot of heartache along the way, Captivate displays a **Submit All** button on each

Question Slide instead of a Submit button. If the learner answers a question and clicks Next (without clicking Submit All), Captivate allows the learner to go to the next question. However, on the last question, if the learner clicks Next, an alert dialog box opens that encourages the learner to Submit All answers.

The **Show Progress** option inserts a counter on each Question slide so that learners know where they are in the quiz.

Allow Backward Movement allows learners to go backward through the quiz.

When you select **Show score at the End of the Quiz**, Captivate adds an additional slide to the project that summarizes how learners score on the quiz.

The **Allow User to Review the Quiz** option allows learners to go back and see how they answered the questions. However, once the answers are submitted for scoring, learners are not able to change their answers.

Note: I didn't cover all of the options in the Quiz Settings dialog box. You can learn about the other options by clicking the **Help** link at the bottom of the dialog box. You will typically find a Help link in most of Captivate's dialog boxes.

3. Set the Pass or Fail options for the Quiz.

    ❏ from the **Quiz** category at the left of the dialog box, select **Pass or Fail**

    ❏ from the Pass/Fail Options area, change the **% or more of total points to pass** to **50**

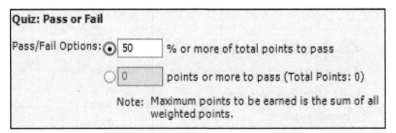

Learners need to correctly answer half of the questions to pass the quiz.

4. Set the Passing and Failing Grade action.

   ❒ from the **Action** drop-down menu for both **If Passing Grade** and **If Failing Grade**, choose **Go to the next slide**

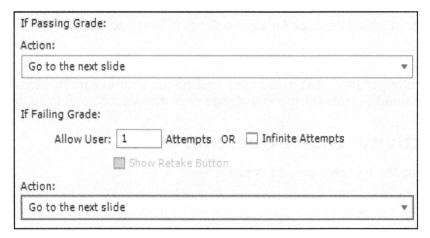

By setting both Actions to **Go to the next slide**, it doesn't matter how learners do on the quiz, they'll end up on next slide on the Filmstrip. You could, however, take learners to a specific slide (or website) should they pass; another should they fail.

   ❒ click the **OK** button

There should be a new slide in the project: Quiz Results. The slide was created because you selected **Show score at the End of the Quiz**.

5. Reposition the Results slide.

   ❒ on the **Filmstrip**, drag the Quiz Results slide down and after the last slide

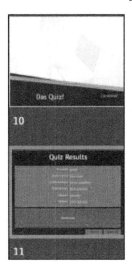

Question Slides

Captivate allows you to add nine different types of Question Slides: Multiple Choice, True/False, Fill-in-the-Blank, Short Answer, Matching, Hot Spot, Sequence, Rating Scale (Likert), and Random Question. All of the Question Slides can be graded (worth a specific number of points) except for Rating Scale (Likert), which is typically used for surveys.

Ideally, any eLearning quizzes you create will be short... no more than 5-10 questions. A quiz longer than that is too long and makes your eLearning lesson all about the quiz instead of transferring knowledge from the lesson to your learner.

Student Activity: Insert Question Slides

1. Ensure that the **QuizMe** project is still open.

2. Insert a Multiple Choice and True/False Question slide.

   ☐ select slide **10**

   ☐ choose **Quiz > Question slide**

   The Insert Questions dialog box appears. If you click the Help link in the lower left of the dialog box, you can read more information about the available question types.

   ☐ from the list of Question Types, select **Multiple Choice**

   ☐ from the list of Question Types, select **True/False**

   ☐ in the field to the right of each question type, ensure that **1** appears

   ☐ from the drop-down menu to the right of each Question type, ensure that **Graded** is selected

   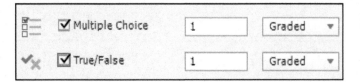

   ☐ click the **OK** button

   Two new slides are added to your project. One contains the Multiple Choice question; the other contains the True/False question.

3. Save your work.

Student Activity: Edit a Question Slide

1. Type a Question and set a Point value.

   ❑ go to slide **11**

   ❑ replace the **Type the question here** text with **Folder names can contain how many characters?**

   ❑ deselect the text box and then resize it as necessary so that it is wide enough to display the text you just typed

2. Type two of the Answers.

   ❑ replace the first **type the answer here** with **9**

   ❑ replace the second **type the answer here** with **255**

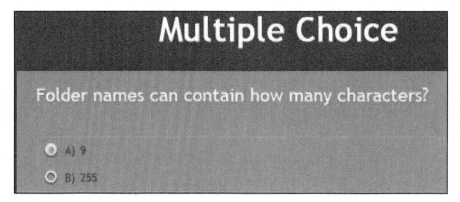

3. Use the Quiz Inspector to add more answers to the question and change its point value.

   ❑ at the far right of the Captivate window, click the **Quiz Inspector**

   ❑ change the number of **Answers** to **4**

   ❑ change the Points to **50**

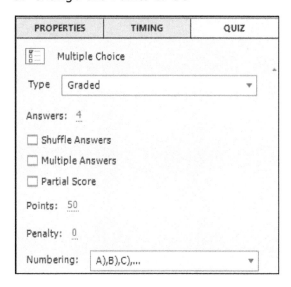

In addition to the question now being worth 50 points, two more answers have been added to the slide.

4. Replace the third "type the answer here" with **8.**

5. Replace the last "type the answer here" with **256.**

6. Specify "B" as the correct answer.

   ☐ click in the circle to the left of **B) 255**

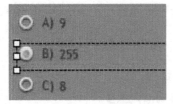

7. Drag the **Answer Area** up a bit (so that the last answer is visible within the orange box).

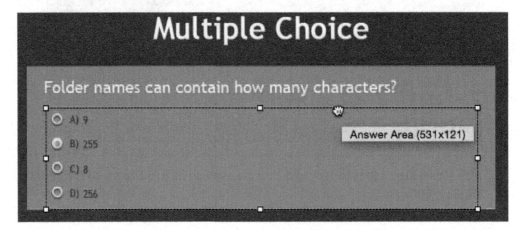

Quiz Confidence Check

1. Edit the True/False question on slide **12** as follows:

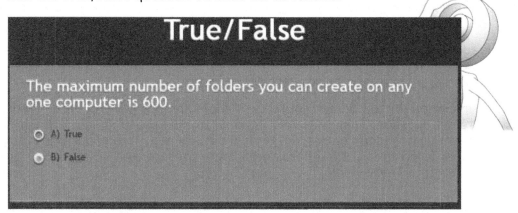

2. On the Quiz Inspector, change the Point value for slide **12** to **50** points.

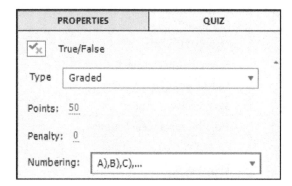

3. Preview the project and take the quiz. (After answering the second question, you will see a Submit All dialog box thanks to the Submit All option you enabled earlier.) Click **Submit All Answers**.

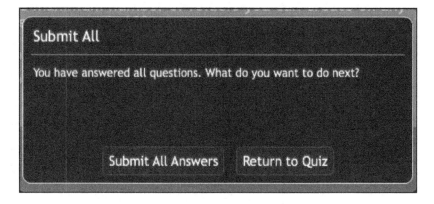

4. When finished, close the preview.

5. Save and close the project.

Knowledge Checks

During this module you learned how to insert graded questions. You can also add Pretest questions (questions with right and wrong answers that can be worth points but are not graded along with regular question slides), and Knowledge Checks.

Once added to a project, Knowledge Check slides behave like any other question slide with a few notable exceptions. As mentioned above, Pretest questions can be worth points; Knowledge Check questions cannot.

In the image on the left below, notice the Actions tab (on the Properties Inspector) for a Pretest question. There are very Actions. In the second image, compare the Actions for a Knowledge Check slide. Simply put, there's more opportunity for you as a developer to ensure your learner is grasping a concept with a Knowledge Check slide than with a Pretest slide.

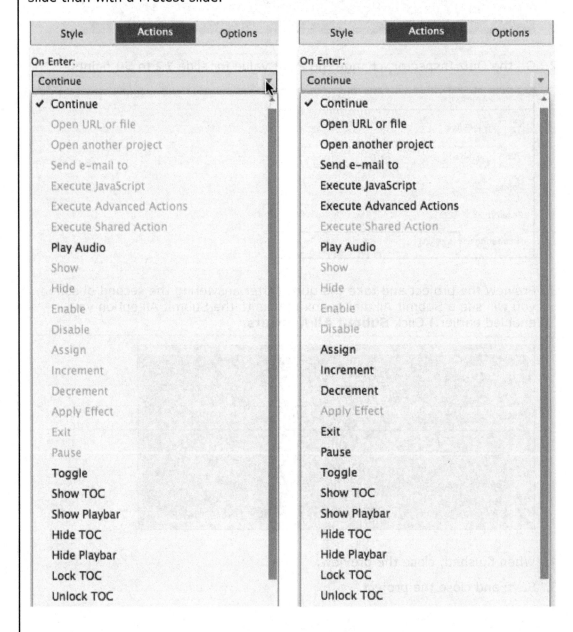

Student Activity: Insert a Knowledge Check

1. Open **KnowledgeMe** from the **Captivate9Data** folder.

2. Insert a Knowledge Check Slide.

   ❑ on the Filmstrip, select slide **1**

   ❑ choose **Quiz > Knowledge Check Slide**

   As with standard quiz questions, the Insert Questions dialog box opens.

   ❑ select **Multiple Choice**

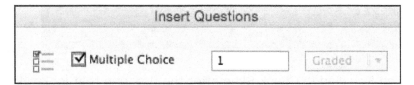

   Notice that the Graded drop-down menu is disabled because Knowledge Checks are not scored.

   ❑ click the **OK** button

   The Knowledge Check slide appears on the Filmstrip just like any other slide. However, notice that the slide includes a graduation cap icon not seen with the other slide types.

Knowledge Check Confidence Check

1. Edit the Knowledge Check Slide as follows:

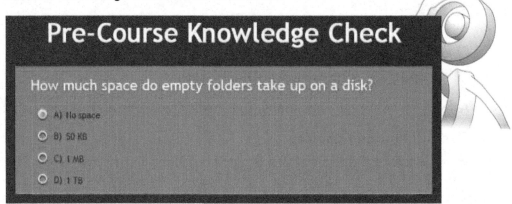

2. Insert a second Knowledge Check Slide after the first one that looks like this:

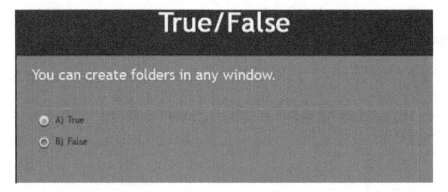

3. Preview the project.

4. When you get to the first Knowledge Check slide, answer the first question incorrectly and click **Submit**.

   You'll be prompted to Try again.

5. Answer the question correctly and click **Submit**.

6. Answer the next question correctly and click **Submit** to begin the main part of the course.

7. Work through the lesson and take the quiz at the end.

   The Quiz Results slide shows you the results of the quiz, but the Knowledge Check results are not included.

8. Close the preview.

9. Save and close the project.

iCONLOGiC
"Skills and Drills" Learning

Module 13: Finishing Touches

In This Module You Will Learn About:

And You Will Learn To:

URL Actions

You learned how to use Click Boxes on page 179 to add interactivity to your projects. But you can use Click Boxes for other purposes. For instance, a Click Box can be used to link an area of a slide to a website or other remote file or to create an email link. And you can use Click Boxes to create links between projects. You'll learn how to create a link to a website next.

Student Activity: Create a Link to a Website

1. Open **FinishMe** from the **Captivate9Data** folder.

2. Insert a Click Box.

   ☐ go to slide **4**

   There is a picture of the Super Simplistic Solutions home page on the slide. You are going to attach a URL to a Click Box that opens the SSS home page in a web browser.

   ☐ choose **Interactions > Click Box**

   A Click Box and three captions are added to the slide.

3. Set the On Success action for the Click Box to open a web page.

   ☐ with the newly inserted Click Box selected, select the **Actions** tab on the Properties Inspector

   ☐ from the **On Success** drop-down menu, choose **Open URL or file**

   ☐ in the URL field, type **http://www.supersimplisticsolutions.com**

4. Force the browser window to appear in a new window and stop the lesson from continuing to play while the learner is on the external web page.

   ☐ click the drop-down menu to the right of the URL that you just typed

❏ choose **New**

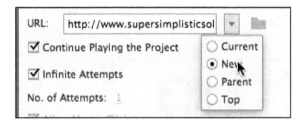

This option forces the link into a new browser window instead of replacing your lesson with the website.

❏ deselect **Continue Playing the Project**

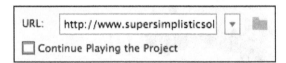

With this option deselected, there is no chance that the eLearning lesson moves on without the learner (until the learner returns to the lesson).

5. Remove the Click Box captions and set other options.

❏ still working on the **Actions** tab of the Properties Inspector, from the **Display** area deselect **Success**, **Failure**, and **Hint**

The Click Box you added is not something that *must* be clicked by the learner, so there is no need to include the feedback captions.

❏ from the **Others** area, select **Hand Cursor**

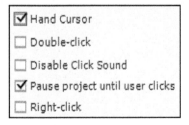

By enabling this option, learners who use the Click Box see a Hand Cursor, a universal sign that the Click Box area is interactive.

❏ ensure that the only other selected option is **Pause project until user clicks**

Without this option, the lesson would end before the learner had a chance to interact with the Click Box.

Click Box Confidence Check

1. Resize the Click Box as necessary so that it covers the website graphic.

2. Preview the project.

3. Test the URL link on slide **4**. (You should be taken to the Super Simplistic Solutions home page.)

4. When finished, close the browser window and the Preview.

5. Save your work.

Skins

Skins perform much the same function for a project as your clothes perform for you. Bored? Bummed? Perhaps something simple like changing your clothes would be enough to change your attitude. Consider some of the top websites in the world. During the holiday season, sites like amazon.com and google.com change the whole attitude of their site just by changing the "skin" used on their sites to reflect the season. The sites themselves don't change; just the outer skin changes.

You are about to learn how easy it is to change the skin used by your project. And you will learn that Skins can be customized to suit your taste—you can select from several playbars, buttons, and color schemes.

Student Activity: Apply a Skin

1. Ensure that the **FinishMe** project is still open.

2. Preview the project and notice that there is a playbar at the bottom of the lesson window. The playbar is just one component of a Skin.

3. Close the preview.

4. Apply a skin to the project.

   ❒ choose **Project > Skin Editor**

   ❒ from the top of the Skin Editor, select the **Playback Control** button

   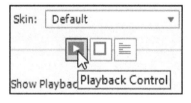

   ❒ from the **Skin** drop-down menu, choose **Pearls**

5. Preview the Project.

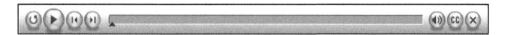

Notice the Pearls skin has been applied to the lesson.

6. Close the preview.

Student Activity: Edit, Save, and Delete a Skin

1. Ensure that the **FinishMe** project is still open.

2. Remove an unnecessary control from the playbar.

   ❏ with the Skin Editor still open (Project or Window menu), ensure **Pearls** is selected from the **Skin** drop-down menu

   ❏ from the lower left of the Skin Editor window, remove the check mark from **Closed Captioning**

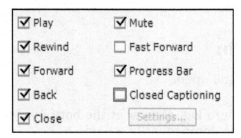

   Because this project does not have any closed captions, the Closed Captioning option is not needed. (Closed Captions are important; they are covered in *Adobe Captivate 9: Beyond the Essentials*.)

3. Save the modifications to the skin as a new skin.

   ❏ click the **Save As** button

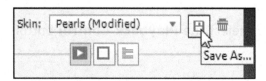

   The Save As dialog box opens.

   ❏ change the name to **Pearls_NoCC**

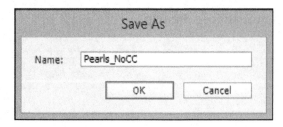

   ❏ click the **OK** button

4. Apply a different skin.

❏ from the Skin drop-down menu, choose **DarkChocolate**

Notice on the preview that the color of your playbar changes to reflect the new skin.

5. Reapply the edited Pearls skin.

❏ from the Skin drop-down menu, choose **Pearls_NoCC**

The preview returns to your selected skin.

6. Delete a skin.

❏ ensure that **Pearls_NoCC** is the selected Skin

❏ click the **Delete** button

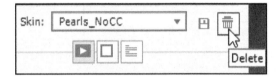

Project Info. Confidence Check

1. Still working in the **FinishMe** project, spend a few moments applying some of the other skins to your project.

2. After you have settled on your favorite skin, preview the project to ensure the skin still meets with your approval.

3. Edit the skin so that it does not use the Closed Captioning option.

4. Save the edited skin with a name that reflects the missing Closed Captioning (such as **name_NoCC**).

5. Close the Skin Editor window.

6. Choose **File > Project Info**.

7. Fill in the information with your personal information (some of the information that you type here will appear on a Table of Contents panel that you are about to create).

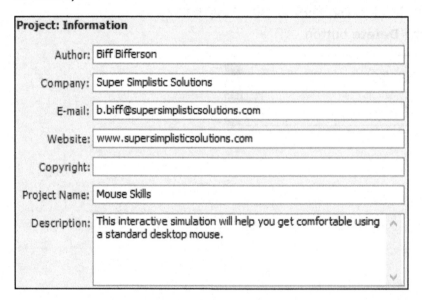

8. Click the **OK** button.

9. Save your work.

Table of Contents

You can create a Table of Contents (TOC) that serves as a navigation aid for your learners. Creating the TOC is as simple as selecting **Show TOC** on the TOC tab of the Skin Editor. A TOC typically appears at the right or left of the lesson, making the lesson wider by a minimum of 250 pixels (something to consider if your lesson is already pretty wide).

Student Activity: Create a TOC

1. Ensure that the **FinishMe** project is still open.

2. Create a TOC.

   ❒ choose **Project > Table of Contents**

   The Skin Editor opens again, but this time you are on the Table of Contents section.

   ❒ from the left side of the Skin Editor, select **Show TOC**

   By selecting Show TOC, an empty TOC has been added to the left of the lesson. Next you will add the four slides in the lesson to the TOC.

   ❒ add check marks to all four slides

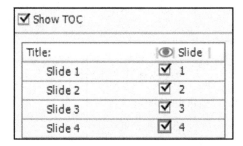

3. Change the slide titles used on the TOC.

   ❒ double-click the current Title for Slide 1

   ❒ replace the current title with the word **Home**

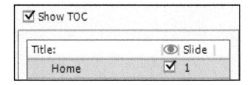

4. Close the Skin Editor window.

5. Save your work.

TOC Confidence Check

1. Still working in the FinishMe project, reopen the Table of Contents window.

2. Change the titles of the remaining slides to match the image below.

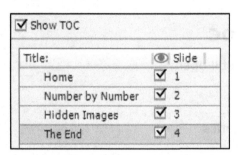

3. Ensure that there is a check mark for each of the slides (as shown above).

4. At the bottom of the Skin Editor, click the **Settings** button.

5. From the **Runtime Options** area, remove the check mark from **Show Topic Duration**.

6. From the **Runtime Options** area, select **Status Flag** (if necessary).

7. Ensure the remaining Runtime Options match the image below and then click the **OK** button.

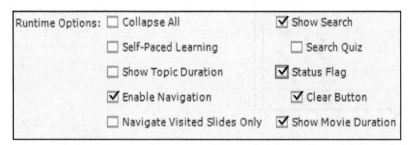

8. Preview the project and notice that the lesson now includes a TOC.

9. As you move through the lesson, check marks are automatically added to the TOC (thanks to the Status Flag option you just selected). *Nice!*

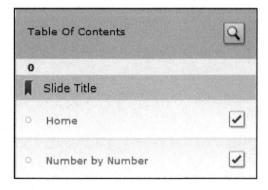

10. Close the preview.

11. Open the Table of Contents window again (if necessary) and from the bottom of the window, click the **Info** button.

12. You added project information earlier (page 218), but the information isn't here. Or is it? Click the **Project Information** button.

    The fields on the TOC information dialog box populate using the project information you added earlier.

13. In the **Photo** area, click the yellow **Browse** folder.

    The Select Image from Library dialog box opens.

14. Click the **Import** button.

15. From the **Captivate9Data/images_animation** folder, open **biff_baby.jpg**.

    You should be back in the main TOC Information dialog box. The name of the image you opened displays in the Photo area.

16. In the Title area, type **Mouse Skills Training**.

17. In the Designation field, type **President**

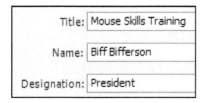

18. Click the **OK** button to close the TOC Information dialog box.

19. Notice in the Preview window at the right that the information and photo appear on the TOC.

20. Close the Skin Editor window.

21. Save your work.

Preloaders

If your learner is using a slow Internet connection and your lesson is large (over 10-15 megabytes), it could take a significant amount of time for the lesson to begin playing on the learner's computer or mobile device. Because most people do not wait for more than a few seconds for something to happen on their device before giving up, a loading screen—an image or message that appears during those first seconds while the initial part of the published lesson is downloading—is critical.

Student Activity: Check Publish Settings and Add a Loading Screen

1. Ensure that the **FinishMe** project is still open.

2. Confirm the Publish Settings.

   ❏ choose **File > Publish Settings**

   ❏ ensure that your Settings match the picture below (all are Captivate defaults)

Project: Publish Settings
Frames Per Second: 30
☐ Publish Adobe Connect metadata.
☑ Include Mouse
☑ Enable Accessibility
☐ Restrict keyboard tabbing to slide items only
☐ Hide selection rectangle for slide items in HTML5
☑ Include Audio
☑ Publish Audio as Mono
☑ Play tap audio for recorded typing
Externalize Resources: ☐ Skin
☐ Widgets
☐ FMR SWF
☐ Animations

Most of the Publish Settings are self-explanatory. However, I'll explain some of the more important options below. (If you want to know more about the options, click the Help link at the bottom of the dialog box.)

Frames Per Second is a measure of how smoothly your published lesson plays. Remember when you were a kid and you made your very own cartoon by drawing a simple stick figure on several pieces of paper? The more pieces of paper you had and the more poses you added to your cartoon character, the more realistic the cartoon looked when you fanned through all of the pieces of paper. The same idea holds true with Frames Per Second. The more frames you have, the smoother your lesson will be. The Captivate default is 30

Frames Per Second, which is plenty. I don't suggest lowering or raising the Frames Per Second unless you are specifically instructed to do so by someone on your team who's in the know. (I've never changed the Frames Per Second in any of my projects.)

Externalize Resources. One goal when publishing your content is to keep the number of published files to a minimum, making file management and uploads to web servers easy. By default, resources such as Skins and Animations are embedded within the published lesson file, resulting in a larger SWF. Unless your SWFs are huge, consider leaving the options as shown on the previous page.

3. Add a loading screen.

   ❏ from the **Project category** at the left, select **Start and End**

   ❏ ensure **Auto Play** is selected from the **Project Start** options area

   With Auto Play selected, the lesson begins playing as soon as it is downloaded by your learner.

   ❏ select **Preloader**

   ❏ click the **Browse** button to the right of Preloader

   You should automatically be browsing the Preloaders folder that comes with Captivate (if not, you can manually browse to the folder via **Gallery\Preloaders**). The Preloader is what the learners see while they are waiting for the lesson to begin playing.

   ❏ from the **Preloaders** folder, open **default loading.gif**

4. Set a Preloader %.

   ❏ change the Preloader % to **50**

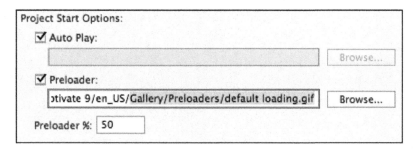

The Preloader % is the percentage of the published Captivate SWF file that must be downloaded to the learner's device before the lesson begins to play. Setting the percentage to 50 percent is pretty standard. I wouldn't suggest going too low (which results in a sputtering playback) or too high (which takes too long for the lesson to begin).

5. Set the project fade options.

   ❏ if necessary, select **Fade In on the First slide**

   ❏ from the **Action** drop-down menu in the **Project End Options** area, ensure **Stop project** is selected

❐ if necessary, deselect **Fade Out on the Last slide**

Fading in on the first slide is a nice effect. However, I've discovered that fading out on the last slide doesn't offer nearly the same impact. In fact, if you leave it selected, you may find that it causes other problems with items on your Timeline that also fade in and/or fade out with objects that pause the slide action. As for the Actions area, I prefer the Stop Project action. When the lesson is finished, it will stop. The learner can then elect to rewind the lesson or close the lesson.

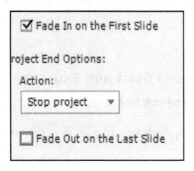

❐ click the **OK** button

6. Save your work.

Publishing

Publishing in Captivate takes your source content and outputs it into a format that can be consumed (viewed) by the learner. Currently, the most common way to publish a Captivate project is as a Flash SWF, an excellent solution because SWF files can be used by the vast majority of the world's personal computers, browsers, and operating systems. Your learners do **not** need Captivate installed on their computer to use an SWF, but they do need a modern web browser and the free Adobe Flash Player (**www.adobe.com**). According to Adobe, the Flash Player is installed on the majority of the world's computers.

Of course, SWFs have a problem. Learners using an Apple mobile device, such as the iPad, iPod, and iPhone (that's millions upon millions of potential learners), cannot use SWF content. Learners using an Apple mobile device who attempt to use an SWF are met with a warning that SWFs are not supported. If you'd like to create content for the Apple mobile devices, all hope is not lost. As an alternative to publishing SWFs, you can publish your content as HTML5. Lessons published as HTML5 play on any computer or mobile device that supports HTML5, including the Apple mobile devices.

If neither SWF nor HTML5 works for you, you can also publish a PDF. However, because PDFs include Flash content, they are not appropriate for devices that do not support Flash (such as the Apple iPad).

> **Note:** Although most features you can add to a Captivate project work when published as HTML5, not all features are supported (such as Rollover Captions and Rollover Images). Prior to publishing as HTML5, you'll use the **HTML5 Tracker** to flag features that are not supported.

Student Activity: Publish as SWF and PDF

1. Ensure that the **FinishMe** project is still open.

2. Specify a Publish format and Project Title.

   ❏ choose **File > Publish**

   The Publish dialog box opens.

   ❏ from **Publish as** drop-down menu, ensure **HTML5/SWF** is selected

   ❏ confirm that the Project Title is **MouseSkills**

   The Project Title ends up being the physical name of the files you publish. Because your published files are likely to be stored on a web server, never use spaces in Project Titles.

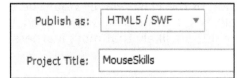

3. Select a Location for the published assets.

   ❏ at the right of the Location field, click the **yellow browse** folder

   ❏ navigate to **Captivate9Data** folder

❏ open the **published_projects** folder

❏ from beneath the Location area, select **Publish To Folder**

The **Publish to Folder** option creates a folder inside the published_projects folder called MouseSkills. There will be occasions when you do not want to create a new folder when publishing—a decision you make on a project-by-project basis.

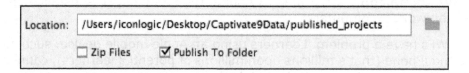

You would typically select **Zip Files** only if you intend to upload your project to an Learning Management System. (Refer to *Adobe Captivate 9: Beyond the Essentials* for more information.) The Fullscreen option causes your published lesson to take over the learner's entire screen; something that most learners do not appreciate.

4. Select the Output Format.

❏ from the **Output Format** area, select **SWF**

The SWF button highlights, indicating it is your selected publish format. The HTML5 should be white. Although you can publish both SWF and HTML5 at the same time, you'll be publishing them separately and then reviewing the files that are physically published.

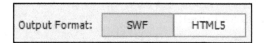

5. Export a PDF and select the Flash Player Version.

❏ from the **Output Format** area, select **Export PDF**

The PDF you create includes all of the lesson's animations, audio, and interactivity. Any learner who has Adobe Reader 9 or newer and the latest Adobe Flash Player can consume your content.

❏ from the Flash Player Version drop-down menu, select **Flash Player 10**

At the time that this book was written, Flash Player 11 was the newest version of the Flash Player. However, if you select a Flash Player version that's too new, learners who have an older version of the Flash Player would be unable to watch your published lesson. By selecting Flash Player 10, or even 10.2, which is more widely used than version 11, it's likely that most learners will be able to view your content.

❏ ensure **Force re-publish on all slides** is selected

With **Force re-publish on all slides**, Captivate refreshes the entire published assets every time you publish a lesson. When you deselect this option, the publish process is quicker. However, every once in a while edited slides do not appear edited in the published version of the lesson.

❐ deselect the other Output options if necessary

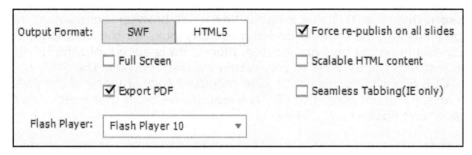

6. Publish the lesson.

❐ click the **Publish** button

Because you selected Export PDF, you are presented with an alert dialog box letting you know that learners need the free Adobe Reader 9 or newer to work with the Flash content within the PDF.

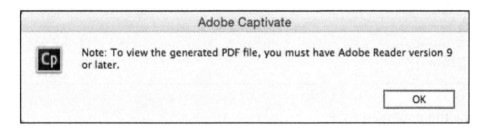

❐ click the **OK** button

Next you are prompted to view the output.

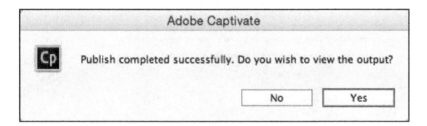

❐ click the **No** button (you'll be previewing both the SWF and the PDF published content in just a moment)

7. Review the assets published to the Publish folder.

❐ minimize (Hide) Captivate and navigate to **Captivate9Data\published_projects**

❐ open the **MouseSkills** folder

The Publish process has yielded a handful of files.

There's an SWF, an HTML file, and a PDF. The SWF contains the lesson, and it's the file learners will be interacting with via a web browser. There is also a JavaScript file (standard.js) and a CSS file (captivate.css). The role of the JS

and CSS files is to ensure that the SWF appears and plays without being blocked by the web browser. And the HTML file is the **start page for the lesson**. Once the HTML file is opened by a web browser, code within the HTML page loads into the browser and immediately looks for the JavaScript and CSS files. Assuming the files are located, more data is added into the HTML page that instructs the SWF file to play within the web browser. *The SWF, HTML, JS, and CSS files should always be kept together. Lose any one of the files, and the lesson will not play.* The PDF is a standalone asset that needs Adobe Reader and Adobe Flash Player.

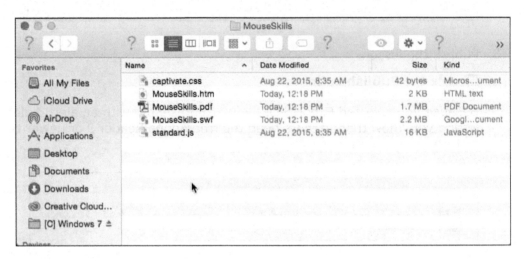

8. View the published SWF.

    ❏ from within the MouseSkills folder, open **MouseSkills.htm**

    The HTML file loads the SWF into your default web browser, and the lesson opens. Keep in mind that learners who attempt to work with an SWF must be on a device that supports SWFs, and they must have a web browser.

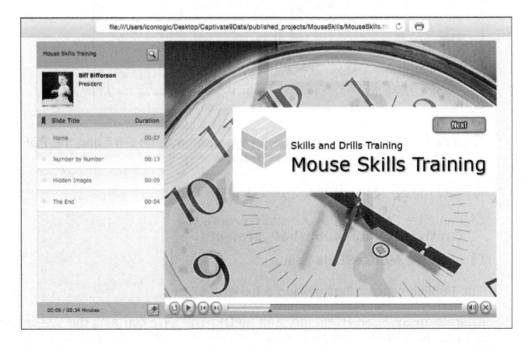

    ❏ close the browser window

9. View the published PDF.

❐ from within the MouseSkills folder, open **MouseSkills.pdf**

The lesson opens just as it did when you opened the HTML file. However, this version of the lesson is running within Adobe Reader or Adobe Acrobat (depending upon what is installed on your computer). The lesson isn't using a web browser but includes all of the rich media (audio, interactivity, and music).

10. Close the PDF and return to the Captivate project.

Student Activity: Run the HTML5 Tracker

1. Ensure that the **FinishMe** project is still open.

2. Test the lesson to see if it is appropriate for HTML5.

   ☐ choose **Project > HTML5 Tracker**

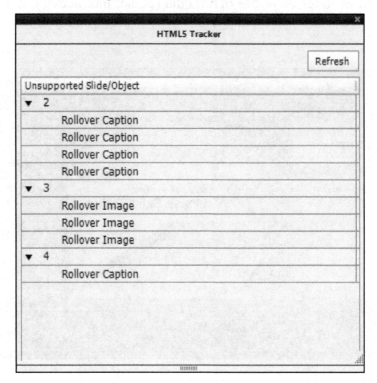

Although this lesson works great on a device that supports Flash (SWFs), HTML5 has limitations. The FinishMe lesson uses Rollover Captions on slides 2, 3, and 4 (you learned how to add Rollover Captions on page 128). For a Rollover Caption to be successful, the learner must use a mouse or touch-pad to literally rollover the Rollover Area. Rollovers on a mobile device aren't just problematic... they're impossible. Although a select few mobile devices can detect movement from a distance, the only way for most mobile users to interact with Rollovers on most devices is to touch the Rollover Area.

Although you could go through and remove the Rollover Captions (possibly replace them with something else) to save time, you will close the project and open another project better suited to be published as HTML5.

3. Close the HTML5 Tracker window.

4. Save and close the FinishMe project.

Student Activity: Publish as HTML5

1. Open **HTML5Me** from the **Captivate9Data** folder.

2. Preview the project.

   This project contains plenty of audio and interactivity. Unlike the last project, it does not contain any Rollover Captions.

3. Test the lesson to see if it is appropriate for HTML5.

   ❒ close the Preview and then choose **Project > HTML5 Tracker**

   This time the results couldn't be better. According to the tracker, you now have a green light to publish the lesson as HTML5.

   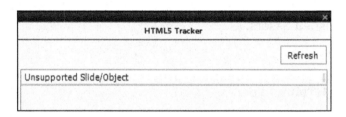

   ❒ close the **HTML5 Tracker** window

4. Specify a Publish format.

   ❒ choose **File > Publish**

   The Publish dialog box opens.

   ❒ from the **Publish as** drop-down menu, ensure **HTML5/SWF** is still selected
   ❒ change the Title to **CreateNewFolder_HTML5**

5. Select a Location for the published assets.

   ❒ at the right of the Location area, click the **yellow browse** folder
   ❒ navigate to **Captivate9Data** folder
   ❒ open the **published_projects** folder and then click the **Select Folder** button (**Choose** on the Mac)

   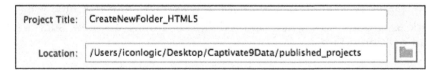

6. Select HTML5 as the Output Format.

   ❒ from the **Output Format** area, deselect **SWF** and select **HTML5**

7. Publish the HTML5 output.

   ❏ click the **Publish** button

   Once the Publish process completes, you are prompted to view the output.

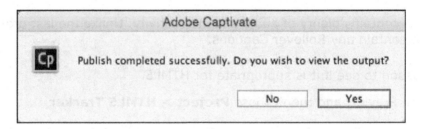

   ❏ click the **No** button (you'll be viewing the content in just a moment)

8. Review the HTML5 published assets.

   ❏ minimize (Hide) Captivate

   ❏ navigate to **Captivate9Data\published_projects** and open the **CreateNewFolder_HTML5** folder

   There are far more assets with the HTML5 output than what resulted from publishing as a SWF. These assets are dependent on each other so everything must be kept together when posted to a web server.

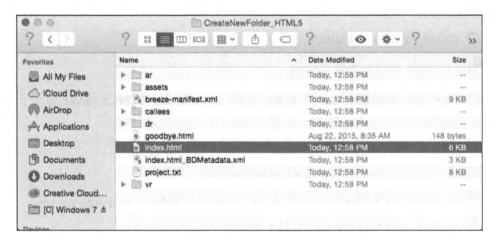

   ❏ open **index** with your web browser to view the lesson

   The lesson plays as expected... it's even interactive. And because it's HTML5, it will work as it does now when opened with a mobile devices, such as the Apple iPad or Kindle Fire.

9. Close the browser.

10. Return to the HTML5Me Captivate project.

Publishing Confidence Check

1. Ensure that the **HTML5Me** project is still open.

   You have learned how to publish projects as SWF (for desktop users) and HTML5 (for mobile users). But which publish format should you ultimately choose? If you publish SWF and then HTML5 separately, you'll have to provide two published lessons for your learners... and require learners to choose the best format.

   Wouldn't it be great if could publish a project as both SWF *and* HTML5, at one time, and let the learner's device (not the learner) ask for the appropriate format based on its capabilities? Sure it would... let's do it.

2. Open the **Publish** dialog box.

3. Change the **Title** to **CreateNewFolder_SWF_HTML5**.

4. From the **Output Format** area, select both **SWF** *and* **HTML5** (enable both options).

5. **Publish** the project (when the Publish process is complete, there's no need to view the Output).

6. Minimize (Hide) Captivate.

7. Navigate to **Captivate9Data\published_projects** and open the **CreateNewFolder_SWF_HTML5** folder.

8. The folder contains a combination of the SWF and HTML5 output files. But there's a new player: **multiscreen.html**.

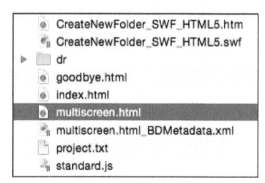

   If you make this file the link for learners to click when accessing the lesson, desktop users who have Flash will automatically be served the SWF version of the lesson. Learners who are using devices that do not support Flash will automatically be served the HTML5 version of the lesson. *How awesome is that?*

9. Return to Captivate.

10. Reopen the **Publish** dialog box.

11. From the Publish as drop-down menu, choose **Video**.

12. Change the Title to **CreateNewFolder_HTML5** and set the publish Location to **Captivate9Data\published_projects**.

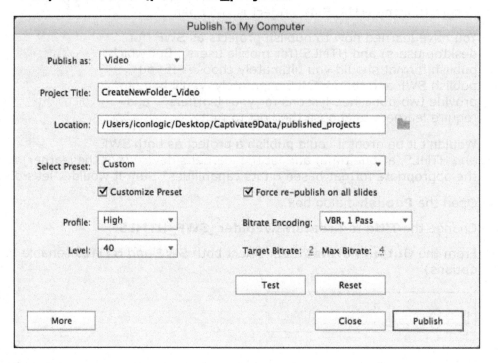

Publish To My Computer

Publish as:	Video ▾
Project Title:	CreateNewFolder_Video
Location:	/Users/iconlogic/Desktop/Captivate9Data/published_projects
Select Preset:	Custom ▾

☑ Customize Preset   ☑ Force re-publish on all slides

Profile:	High ▾
Level:	40 ▾

Bitrate Encoding: VBR, 1 Pass ▾

Target Bitrate: 2   Max Bitrate: 4

Test   Reset

More   Close   Publish

13. Publish the project.

The Adobe Captivate Video Publisher opens and generates a video.

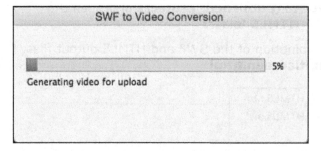

SWF to Video Conversion

5%

Generating video for upload

14. When prompted, **Open the Published Video**.

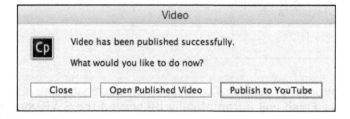

Video

Cp Video has been published successfully.

What would you like to do now?

Close   Open Published Video   Publish to YouTube

The MP4 video will open on just about any device (including desktops, laptops, and mobile devices) and can be uploaded to video services such as YouTube. However, because this is a video, there's no interactivity possible. Throughout the short video, you are prompted to click on the screen, but you aren't able to comply. Keep the no-interactivity issue in mind when developing your eLearning lessons. Although videos are perfectly fine, they may not meet your training needs.

15. Close the video and the Adobe Captivate Video Publisher.

16. Choose **File > Print**.

    The Print dialog box is a bit misleading. You can't actually print your Captivate slides from here. However, you can Publish your project as a Microsoft Word document and then print from Word.

17. Ensure that the **Export range** is set to **All**.

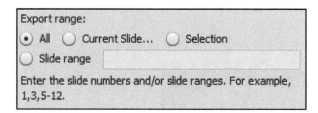

18. From the **Type** drop-down menu, choose **Handouts**.

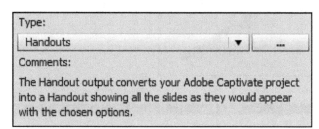

19. From the **Handout Layout Options** area, deselect **Use table in the output**.

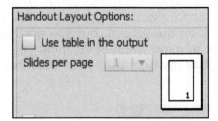

20. Select **Caption Text**.

21. Select **Add blank line for notes**.

22. Select **Include objects and questions**

    The four remaining options should be deselected.

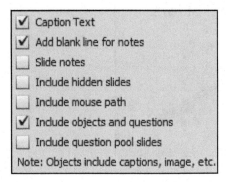

23. Publish the document and View the Output.

    The handout opens in Microsoft Word. Similar to PowerPoint, the document can be printed and serve as support material for your lesson.

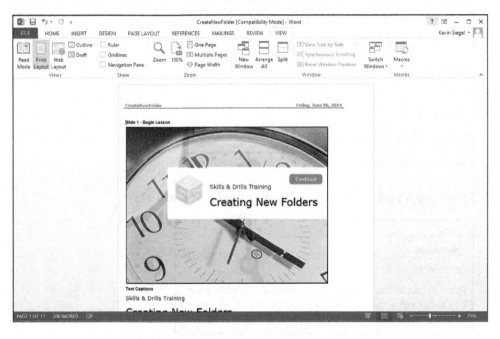

24. Close the Word document and return to Captivate.

Round Tripping

Exporting captions to Microsoft Word is one of my favorite Captivate features. Why? If you export the captions to Word, any team member can open the exported document with Word and make editorial changes. Those changes can be *imported into Captivate*—something I call **Round Tripping**.

You can use this round trip workflow to create multiple-language versions of your project without having to rerecord or re-create the project. All you have to do is send the exported captions to an interpreter and have the caption text translated into another language. You would then import the translated captions into your project. *Cool!*

Student Activity: Export Captions to Microsoft Word

1. Ensure that the **HTML5Me** project is still open.

2. Export the project captions.

   ❑ choose **File > Export > Project Captions and Closed Captions**

   The Save As dialog box opens.

   ❑ ensure that you are saving to the **Captivate9Data** folder as **HMTL5Me Captions**

   ❑ click the **Save** button

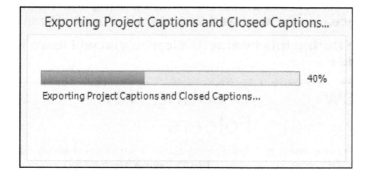

You are notified when the captions have been exported.

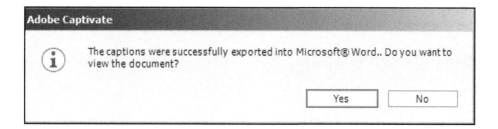

   ❑ click the **Yes** button to open the Word document

The captions have been imported into a Word table. There are five columns with the following headers: **Slide Id**, **Item Id**, **Original Text Caption Data**, **Updated Text Caption Data**, and **Slide**. You can make any changes you want to the Updated Text Caption Data, but you must not change any of the

other information. The slide ID identifies to which slide your edited captions go. The Item ID identifies which caption goes with which caption data.

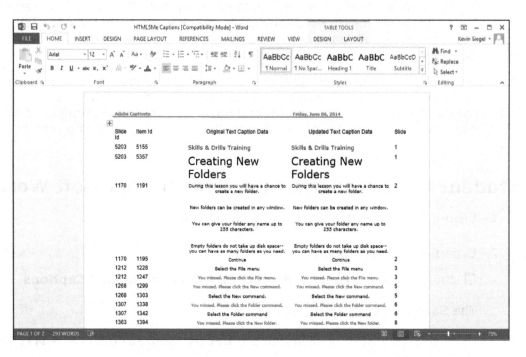

3. Update the Word content.

   ❑ on slide ID **1170**, Item ID **1191**, find the phrase **During this lesson you will have a chance...** in the **Updated Text Caption Data** column

   ❑ change the text to **During this interactive lesson you will learn how to create a new folder.**

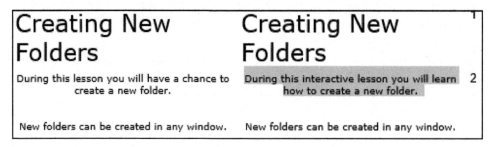

4. Save the Word document and close Microsoft Word.

5. Return to the Captivate project.

Student Activity: Perform a Round Trip

1. Ensure that the **HTML5Me** project is still open.

2. Import the edited caption into the Captivate project.

   ❏ choose **File > Import > Project Captions and Closed Captions**

   The Open dialog box appears.

   ❏ open **HTML5Me Captions** from the **Captivate9Data** folder

   You will be notified that the items were imported into the project.

   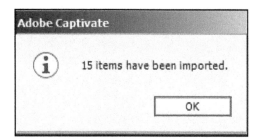

   ❏ click the **OK** button

3. Review the updated caption.

   ❏ go to slide **2**

   Notice that the text you changed in the Word document has been updated on the slide. How awesome is that?

   During this interactive lesson you will learn how to create a new folder.

   New folders can be created in any window.

   You can give your folder any name up to 255 characters.

   Empty folders do not take up disk space you can have as many folders as you need.

4. Save your work and close the project.

   And a hearty congratulations are in order... you have completed this book. There's much more to Captivate of course (see the next page), but you should now feel comfortable creating new projects and recording screen actions. You should be able to add standard objects such as click boxes, buttons, text entry boxes, images, characters, videos, and animations. And you should feel comfortable in your ability to not only Publish your content but create output files appropriate for the kind of device you expect your learners to be using.

Want More Captivate? Need Help?

By completing the lessons in this book, you have learned the essential skills that enable you to immediately create effective soft skills learning, demonstrations, and simulations in Adobe Captivate.

If you'd like to go beyond the basics and learn even more about Captivate, consider *Adobe Captivate 9: Beyond the Essentials*.

Topics covered in *Adobe Captivate 9: Beyond the Essentials* include, but are not limited to, the following:

- ❏ Project Templates & Custom Themes
- ❏ Master Slides
- ❏ Custom Object Styles
- ❏ Project Import/Branching
- ❏ Question Pools
- ❏ Responsive Projects
- ❏ Widgets
- ❏ Variables
- ❏ Aggregator Projects
- ❏ Advanced Actions
- ❏ LMS Integration

If you would like to learn more about *Adobe Captivate 9: Beyond the Essentials*, visit **http://www.iconlogic.com**.

Captivate Support

We are happy to provide one-on-one consulting, mentoring, and turn-key development services for all versions of Adobe Captivate. We also offer one-on-one reviewing and editing of your technical documents and projects. You can learn about our services via our website: **http://www.iconlogic.com**.

Index

ISBN 1-932733-84-1

9 781932 733846

5 3 9 0 0

Adobe Captivate 9: The Essentials

CPSIA information can be obtained
at www.ICGtesting.com
Printed in the USA
LVOW05s0718020416

481897LV00005B/13/P